# BRADDOCK

## THE RISE OF THE CINDERELLA MAN

### Jim Hague

ROBSON BOOKS

This paperback edition first published in Great Britain in 2005 by Robson Books,
The Chrysalis Building, Bramley Road, London W10 6SP

An imprint of **Chrysalis** Books Group plc

First published in the USA by Chamberlain Bros., a member of Penguin Group
(USA) Inc. in 2005

British Library Cataloguing in Publication Data
A catalogue record for this title is available from the British Library.

ISBN 1 86105 891 8

Printed in Italy
Original book design by Mike Rivilis

While the author has made every effort to provide accurate Internet addresses at the
time of publication, neither the publisher nor the author assumes any responsibility
for errors, or for changes that occur after publication.

# Foreword

James J. Braddock, eventually known by the nickname of "The Cinderella Man," a name given to him by the legendary sportswriter Damon Runyon, was the classic fairytale boxing hero, the quintessential underdog, long before Rocky Balboa was popularized on the silver screen, long before Chuck Wepner, Leon Spinks and James "Buster" Douglas became household names because of their surprising boxing exploits.

Braddock became an everyman hero at a time when America desperately needed one. He came back from the depths of financial despair during the Great Depression to earn the biggest accolade a professional boxer could: the title of heavyweight champion of the world. He earned his place in boxing history by pulling off perhaps the greatest upset in the history of the sport, becoming living proof that anything really could happen in the world of sports; that nothing was impossible.

Braddock lived a simple life. He became a devoted family man, a loving husband, a loyal friend. He was beloved by all. In a sport that inspired fear, brought images of violence and anger, Braddock was the opposite: a genuinely nice man who earned his place among sports legends because of pugilism, even though he had only reluctantly made it a part of his lifestyle.

His life story is the stuff that movies are made of, which is why it shouldn't surprise anyone that *The Cinderella Man*, a biography-picture starring Academy Award winners Russell Crowe and Renée Zellweger and directed by Oscar-winning director Ron Howard, is currently scheduled for release.

Braddock's saga is also compelling enough to put to words, from his humble beginnings growing up dirt-poor in New York, to 1974, when he died in his sleep at his home in North Bergen, New Jersey at the age of 68.

This is an attempt to chronicle the life of "the Cinderella Man," perhaps the least likely of all boxers to hold the title of heavyweight champion of the world.

# 1

The late spring, and early summer of 1906 were particularly hot, with temperatures regularly reaching the high 80s before the first official days of summer. It was quite rare to experience such weather in the early days of June, but New York City was sweltering on June 7, the temperature hovering around 92 degrees, when an Irish immigrant named Elizabeth O'Toole Braddock went into labour with her fifth child, about to contribute further to a family that would still see the birth of two more infants.

Joseph Braddock, another Irish immigrant, was your typical hardworking provider, dividing his time between three jobs (security guard, pier watchman and furniture mover) in order to keep his large family fed and a roof over their heads in a small apartment on West 48th Street in Manhattan.

It was in that flat that Elizabeth Braddock gave birth to the largest of her five boys and two girls, this one a whopping 17-pound baby boy that the couple named James.

The idea of any woman giving birth to a healthy 17-pound infant at the time was unthinkable, especially without the assistance of a midwife. But the strong-willed Elizabeth Braddock wanted no help in bringing a child into the world. She did it on her own, requesting only several blocks of ice to cool the small bedroom down.

On that very same day, the RMS *Lusitania*, a passenger cruise ship, was launched for the first time across the Atlantic Ocean. The *Lusitania* was the largest vessel afloat at the time and became a very popular mode of transportation from London to New York for the aristocracy for the next nine years.

Unfortunately, in 1915, the *Lusitania* was sunk off the coast of Ireland by a torpedo fired by a German submarine, and 1,201 passengers drowned. The sinking of the *Lusitania* and the tragic loss of lives sparked a public outcry that raised tensions between Germany and the United States and helped create the climate in which the U.S. entered World War I.

Also on the same day that James Walter Braddock (his middle initial was changed to J. by a manager when he became a professional boxer) was brought into the world, the Chicago Cubs scored 11 runs in the first inning off Hall of Fame pitcher Christy Mathewson of the New York Giants at the start of what became an unthinkable 19-0 rout. It remains the Cubs franchise record for runs scored in a first inning and it is especially impressive because it came at the expense of perhaps the greatest pitcher of the era.

Only a few months after his son James was born, Joseph Braddock realized that a small Manhattan apartment was not a good setting to raise a family of five children, so he decided to cross the Hudson River to New Jersey, like many other Irish immigrants—and Italians as well—had done before him.

New Jersey was not as densely populated as Manhattan. The cost of living was much lower. Joseph Braddock figured he would be able to purchase a home for his family while remaining directly across the river from New York. Braddock took his wife and kids to the town of West New York, New Jersey, where the Braddock family would remain for several years.

West New York provided a safe haven for the Braddocks. They fitted in well with their new surroundings, and young Jimmy made a lot of friends right away. He was a friendly kid, well liked, with an upbeat personality. Because he was so much bigger than most of the kids his age, a lot of the other kids in the streets of West New York either gravitated toward him or shied away from him; some feared him even though he was such a lovable kid.

Jimmy Braddock was enrolled in St. Joseph of the Palisades grammar school in West New York. As a youngster, he loved to play marbles, a game at which he became very proficient. But baseball was his favorite sport by far. He would play at the neighborhood parks as often as possible.

In the early 1910s, there were really only three sports of note: baseball, boxing and thoroughbred horse racing. In his early days, young Jimmy Braddock concentrated on becoming a baseball star. In fact, he concentrated more on baseball than he did on his studies at St. Joseph. Jimmy also spent a lot of his time swimming in the Hudson River or under the Hackensack River Bridge at the North Bergen-Secaucus border.

When it came to academics, Braddock wasn't the greatest. It didn't help that he had more than his share of run-ins with school authority figures and found himself getting into trouble.

One of the first friends that Braddock played with regularly in his early childhood days was a skinny Italian kid named Orlando Carmelo Scarnecchia, who had moved to West New York from Ohio right around the time that the Braddock family relocated there.

Later in life, the skinny Italian kid from Ohio became known as John Scarne, one of the most famous and celebrated magicians of his time.

In his 1966 memoir, *The Odds Against Me*, Scarne admitted that the first thing he wanted to become in life was a professional boxer, and that he would regularly spar—and of course, lose—against Jimmy Braddock.

However, Scarne wrote in his book that he would beat Braddock at checkers as often as Braddock defeated the master magician at boxing.

Around that time, Braddock inadvertently and reluctantly began his boxing career—fighting with his classmates at St. Joseph.

Because of his size—he towered over most of his classmates—Braddock would find himself either getting lured into fights with other classmates or having to protect some of his friends from those who would try to bully them. Braddock was like the master protector, the big brother of the neighbourhood, an image even further enhanced through Braddock's older brother, Joseph Jr., who wanted to pursue a career in boxing.

Being Irish American and being interested in boxing almost became synonymous at that time. Boxing was a way of life for many Irishmen, as natural an activity for many as expressing their opinions, and as enjoyable as drinking whiskey or cold beer. The best-known Irish-Americans of the era were boxing champions, like the bare-fisted John L. Sullivan, and later on, Jack Dempsey and Mickey Walker.

Boxing was a way for the hardworking Irish not only to make a name for themselves, but also to make some money on the side. Whereas some kids aspired to be doctors or lawyers, policemen or firemen, a lot of young Irish kids at the time wanted to become prizefighters.

Young Jimmy Braddock got his first taste of pugilism in grade school, when fighting was just another social activity. It became as commonplace in West New York as baseball. Kids wanted to act like their favourite boxers, and they had the opportunity to do so practically every day after school.

In those grade-school years, Braddock had one particular nemesis—an older, bigger kid named Jimmy Morris. The two had a running feud with each other and tangled more than thirty times. Records of those brawls aren't easily located, so it is not known who had the upper hand in those school-day fisticuffs, but in his adult years, Braddock would later be quoted as saying that his fights with Jimmy Morris in the schoolyards of St. Joseph were some of the toughest he ever had.

"That Morris kid was one tough kid," Braddock told a sportswriter in 1933. "He wouldn't go away. He kept coming back for more and more. He also was the first one to ever hurt me. He might have been the first one to break my nose, but I'm not so sure."

Braddock also remembered the first kid he knocked out: another St. Joseph student by the name of Elmer Furlong.

By the age of 14, Jimmy Braddock had had his fill of schooling. He had an opportunity to get a job, working as a printer's assistant in a print shop in New York, so without telling his parents, he quit St. Joseph to take the job, and made anywhere between $7 and $10 per week, depending on sales and tips.

Although Braddock told friends that he aspired to become a fireman or a train engineer, the big kid with the powerful right hand was simply destined to become a fighter.

However, there was no way anyone back then could have ever predicted the remarkable journey that Braddock would travel as soon as he laced up the gloves and shoes for the very first time.

When his older brother Joseph Jr. had fought nineteen professional bouts, he encouraged Jimmy to take up the sport. With his brother as his trainer, James Braddock launched his amateur career at the age of 17.

*James Braddock. (AP Photo)*

# 2

Joseph Braddock, Jr. was nowhere near as big as his brother, the eventual heavyweight champion, but he was also a strapping young man with a powerful punch. Joseph became a professional boxer after having worked his way through the amateur ranks. He won 16 of 19 professional bouts before having to walk away from boxing because of injuries and illness.

But seeing the punch that his little brother possessed, Joseph encouraged Jimmy to enter the ring himself. Joe Braddock told his brother that he would work with him, teaching him everything he knew. He would be his first handler and trainer. It would be a perfect family arrangement, because Joe Braddock was never going to allow anyone to mess with his little brother—even though by this time Jimmy Braddock could handle himself quite well.

During his teenage years, Jimmy Braddock had already been through a handful of jobs, from the printer's apprenticeship in Manhattan to working as a messenger boy for Western Union, an errand boy for a silk mill in neighbouring Guttenberg, and a general dockworker and lorry driver, when his brother suggested that he seriously consider becoming a boxer.

At six-foot-three, Braddock was lean, weighing 150 pounds at most, so his first venture into the world of boxing was to be as a middleweight at the tender age of seventeen. Joe Braddock knew that his brother with his lanky frame and powerful right hand, had a bright future in the fight game. So did others who saw him box even as a raw and unproven fighter. They knew that Jimmy Braddock was lightning in a bottle, blessed with a natural ability and thunderous right hand that only came along once or twice in a generation. The right hand he had first showed off to the students at St. Joseph was about to be unleashed in rings across the state of New Jersey.

On November 27, 1923, in a Grantwood, New Jersey (later Cliffside Park) gymnasium, Jimmy Braddock entered the ring for the first time, fighting under the alias of Jimmy Ryan (lots of fighters used aliases, either to protect their ranking or for marketing purposes). He took on a Fort Lee police officer by the name of Tommy Hummel. Both fighters showed their inexperience and pummeled each other from the outset. Newspaper reports said that both Braddock and Hummel hit the canvas "several times" during the course of the fight, and that Hummel was the winner of the bout; they also reported that it was certainly the most entertaining fight of the night.

It was enough of a taste to whet Braddock's appetite for pursuing boxing more intently.

Through his connections in the fight game, Joe Braddock started to line up amateur fights for his brother. It didn't take long for both of them to see that they had made the right choice. Jimmy Braddock was well on his way to a fine career in the ring.

Braddock remained a successful amateur fighter for three years, moving up the ranks and fighting more than 100 bouts. He eventually became the New Jersey light-heavyweight and heavyweight amateur champion, winning the titles in successive seasons (1925 and 1926). He went an amazing 38 straight amateur fights without a loss, an accomplishment almost unthinkable at the time. He was being touted as a possible contender, even though he was still young and inexperienced. There was one thing for sure: Jimmy Braddock was a rising star.

Conquering the amateur game was one thing. Turning professional was another. A lot of the amateurs back then were boxing as a hobby and had no aspirations to turn professional. Some amateurs in the early 1920s were in their 30s and even 40s when they climbed into the ring against the long, lanky teenager from West New York. Some were out of shape and unskilled. They represented ethnic clubs and athletic clubs, even neighbourhoods and towns.

There was no denying Braddock's background whenever he fought. His wardrobe told the tale of his proud Irish heritage. He wore a green robe with a white shamrock on the back when he entered the ring, then when it came time to fight, he took off the robe to reveal white satin shorts with a green shamrock on the right leg.

The shamrock became synonymous with Braddock. In fact, some writers at the time wanted to give Braddock a catchy nickname to capitalize on his ancestry. One New Jersey-based writer tried to label him "Irish" Jim Braddock, but the name never caught on. Another wanted to call him "Gentleman" Jim Braddock, like another Irish boxing great long before him, "Gentleman" Jim Corbett. In fact, James Walter Braddock did become James J. Braddock after turning professional to mirror the name of James J. Corbett. But "Gentleman Jim" never quite fit Braddock. "Jersey James" was another nickname that was bantered about and eventually utilized by famed *New York Times* sportswriter John Kiernan.

He'd receive a moniker by another sportswriter later in life that would remain with him forever.

In early 1926, the Braddock brothers were approached by a shrewd ring man who spotted Jimmy Braddock when he was working down at the docks on the Hoboken waterfront. His name was Joe Gould. Gould was a New York City guy of modest means, who had made a little bit of money selling candy on the railroad, while always being fascinated by the fight game. He'd spent a lot of time around boxing gyms and athletic clubs. He always wanted to learn more about boxing, about managing and training. He was a veteran of World War I, having served in the U.S. Navy, and he got his start in the sport by putting on boxing shows while on duty.

Gould had also started to book and promote fights near where he was stationed in Newport, Rhode Island. He knew talent when he saw it, and he recognized it in Braddock without ever seeing him in the ring. Gould saw size and strength on the docks, and taking one look at Braddock's already mangled nose, he knew that the kid had been in his share of scrapes already.

"There was always just something special about that boy," Gould would later say. "He stood out like a sore thumb. There was something about me being drawn to him, like it was supposed to happen."

Gould was knowledgeable when it came to boxing, an insightful, keen strategist who could disarm an opponent by picking up on tendencies in the blink of an eye. He told the Braddock brothers that he could work with Jimmy and turn him into a good professional boxer. The elder Braddock would handle the training out of Joe Jeanette's gym in Hoboken, Gould would be the manager, and the rest would be up to the kid with the powerful right.

So, in March, 1926, after mastering the amateur boxing world, the time had come for Jimmy Braddock to begin his professional career. He wasn't about to give up his job working on the docks, because he was making good money. But a boxing career would provide a strong supplementary income, especially for a young star on the rise. Braddock's professional career began as a middleweight; he weighed all of 160 pounds.

Although there are some published reports that state Braddock's first professional fight took place on January 28, 1927 against George LaRocco, that is inaccurate. In fact, Braddock had 16 professional fights, all in an eight-month span of 1926, before facing LaRocco on the aforementioned date.

Gould arranged for Braddock to fight Al Settle in Hoboken on April 14, 1926. It was a pretty inauspicious debut, especially for someone with Braddock's Golden Gloves amateur background. The fight ended in a four-round no decision.

Gould wasted no time putting his young prodigy back into the ring. Just eight days later, on April 22, Braddock fought George Deschner in Ridgefield Park, New Jersey and knocked him out in the second round. Braddock had his first professional knockout.

That victory started a streak of sorts. In May of 1926, Braddock fought three times and won all three with first-round knockouts. The last fight of the month was in a crowded bingo hall in Wilkes-Barre, Pennsylvania, where Braddock was on the undercard of a 10-bout boxing smorgasbord. Willie Daily was a crusty older opponent, a true club fighter from the steel mills of Pennsylvania. It might have been a tough match for some young fighters, but Jimmy Braddock's powerful right hand prevailed.

In June, Braddock returned to the ring to face Leo Dobson in Jersey City. Again, he won with a first-round knockout. Braddock had won five straight fights as a pro, four in a row via a knockout in the first round. His reputation began to grow rapidly.

On July 9, 1926, Braddock faced his toughest foe to date in Walter Westman, who had developed his own reputation as a banger and a brawler. The two went toe-to-toe for the first two rounds, but Braddock severely bloodied Westman in the third and the match was stopped, with Braddock earning a technical-knockout victory. He was now 6-0 with one no-decision. The future was as bright as Gould had envisioned it.

In August and September, there was a string of five straight early knockouts, four of which came in the first round. Fans in Braddock's native West New York were treated to seeing their hometown hero twice in a span of 14 days in September, and Braddock didn't disappoint, defeating Ray Kennedy (on the 16th) and Carmine Caggiano (on the 30th) in first-round knockouts.

Braddock's record was stellar: 11 wins, all via knockout, eight of which had come in the first round. He was quickly getting a large following.

Seizing the opportunity for a local boy on the rise, Gould was able to get his fighter into the Mecca of professional boxing, Madison Square Garden.

"I was lucky enough to get a break in the Garden a couple of times," Braddock himself said in the book, *In This Corner*, written by Peter Heller, which featured interviews with many of the all-time boxing greats.

"Once I got into the Garden, I had to make the most of my chance," said Braddock. "I knew a lot of guys from Jersey would come over to watch me, so I didn't want to disappoint them. I thought I was a pretty good puncher at the time, but they rated me as a boxer-puncher, not as a knockout puncher."

On November 12, 1926, the undefeated Braddock fought Lou Barba in a six-round middleweight fight at the Garden as part of the undercard of another big 10-bout night. It was Braddock's toughest fight to date. The two battled each other tooth and nail; Braddock finally took control in the later rounds and won a hard-earned decision, much to the delight of the throng of faithful from Hudson County that had journeyed across the Hudson to see their beloved Jimmy.

Three weeks later, Braddock had a score to settle—with none other than Al Settle, the same fighter he'd battled to a no-decision in his professional debut. This time, there was no question who would be the winner. Braddock won an easy six-round decision, improving his professional record to 13-0.

Braddock won his next bout with a six-round decision over Joe Hudson in Madison Square Garden. He then fought Doc Conrad to a four-round no-decision in Jersey

City on December 20, finishing the first year of his professional boxing life with an impressive 14-0 record with two no decisions, all in just eight months.

Braddock's reputation was growing, and it was only a matter of time before he would get his shot at the big time.

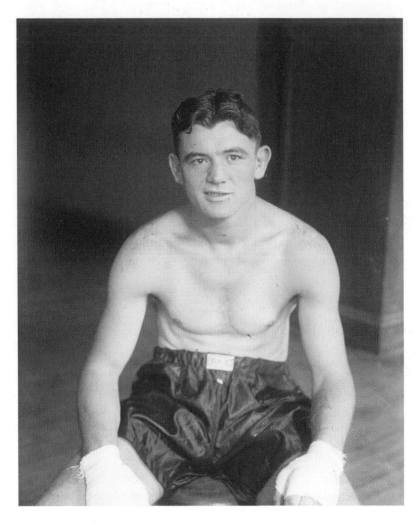

*James J. Braddock, training for future bouts, is shown seated in 1929. (Photo © Bettmann/CORBIS )*

# 3

n 1927, the promoters at Madison Square Garden believed that Braddock was such a local draw that they moved him up the card a little, making him more of a headliner than an undercard specialist. They also believed that he was ready to take on tougher opponents, so they set him up against another up-and-comer named George LaRocco as one of the premier bouts on the evening of January 28.

"He was a pretty good attraction," Braddock said in Heller's book. "But I knocked him out." And in the first round at that.

"I guess you can say I was coming on," Braddock said at the time. He was coming on so quickly that he decided to give up his job in the Hoboken shipping docks to concentrate full-time on boxing. He could finally afford to do so. The prize money was far better than any salary he could receive down at the docks. He had become a true professional.

Braddock returned to his familiar stomping grounds of Wilkes-Barre for his next two fights of 1927, defeating Johnny Alberts in a fourth-round knockout and then disposing of Jack Nelson in a six-round decision two weeks later. Although Braddock was still a middleweight, both he and Gould knew that it was only a matter of time before Braddock moved up. The purses were bigger in both the light-heavyweight and heavyweight divisions. It's where all the attention, glamour and prestige were. But to take on the light heavyweights, he would have to add some meat to his 160-pound frame, which was never easy.

"I was always looking to put on that extra ten pounds," Braddock told Heller. "But I never could attain that."

In March of 1927, Braddock fought twice in five days, defeating both Lou Barba and Nick Fadil to improve to 19-0 before taking his first step up the weight chain. He fought three times in the light-heavyweight (177-pound) class, while weighing nearly 20 pounds less than each opponent, between March and May of 1927. It seemed to make no difference to Braddock, who won all three fights in early knockouts. His first test in the new division came right at home in West New York on May 11 against a journeyman fighter named Jack Stone. Braddock defeated Stone in a tough 10-round decision. Nine days later, he locked horns with his rival George LaRocco again in their second fight of the calendar year in Madison Square Garden. This time, LaRocco was a tougher challenge for Braddock, who had to gut out a bruising six-round decision.

The third win came against a promising brawler namely Stanley Simmons in Jersey City on May 2, 1927.

Some experts had believed that the crafty Simmons might pose a problem for Braddock, because he was much shorter and stockier. Simmons was supposed to be able to get under the statuesque Braddock and hurt him with body punches. But Braddock was much quicker than the plodding Simmons and pummeled him with a series of rights that ended the fight in the first round. When it was over, Simmons didn't know what had hit him or where he was.

"I can't believe how hard that bum hit me," Simmons told a reporter after the fight. "I had never been hit like that by anything, man or machine."

It is amazing that the boxers of that era were able to recover from the constant pounding that they endured and climb back into the ring within a matter of days, not months like the boxers of today. Braddock and his contemporaries even used much lighter gloves with much less protection for their hands. As a result, Braddock suffered through his share of hand injuries, the effects of which would remain with him for the rest of his life.

Braddock fought three more light-heavyweight exhibitions in the spring of 1927, facing Paul Cavalier in

Arcola Park, New Jersey and then his friend Jimmy Francis in both West New York and Union City. These bouts helped prepare him for his third and final go-round with LaRocco, which was set for Madison Square Garden in July.

Francis was always a formidable sparring partner and a close friend to Braddock, on call whenever the popular fighter needed to work out or put on a good show for an adoring audience. At that time, it was commonplace to see a popular fighter stage a workout or an exhibition, solely with the intent of receiving a portion of the gate.

Because Braddock was gaining popularity among his hometown fans, he would conduct the exhibitions as a way for the locals to see him in action at a far lower admission price than they would have to pay at Madison Square Garden—perhaps 15 to 25 cents, whereas a ticket to the Garden would be over a dollar.

Braddock defeated LaRocco in a six-round decision. After he'd defeated Joe Monte in a 10-round decision on October 5, James J. Braddock had a professional record of 25-0 with 16 knockouts.

Babe Ruth may have been the only professional athlete to have a better year in 1927 than Jimmy Braddock. While Ruth was smashing 60 homers for the New York Yankees team whose lineup became known as "Murderers' Row," Braddock was pure murder on his opponents in the ring, beginning the year as the fourteenth-ranked light-heavyweight in the world by *The Ring* magazine.

Braddock was feeling good about his place in the boxing world as 1928 began. His reputation was growing, and he was earning good money and investing it wisely in the stock market. Braddock was 21 years old and single, and he still had his boyish Irish face, although it was beginning to show the wear of 25 professional fights and a handful of exhibitions and no-decisions. He was sitting almost at the top of the boxing world. Almost.

Braddock began the new year with an eight-round victory over Paul Swiderski in New York on January 6, 1928, but then he took the next five months off, recovering from his first serious injury, a broken right hand. He wouldn't be able to keep up the hectic schedule that he had maintained through his first two years of fighting.

After the injury healed, Braddock went back to the gym to get ready for his next match, a May 7 light-heavyweight fight against contender Jack Darnell in Jersey City. Braddock knocked Darnell out in the fourth round, extending his undefeated streak. Things were looking very good for the powerful Irishman from West New York.

But then Gould signed on for a rematch against Joe Monte, the same finesse fighter that Braddock had defeated in a 10-round decision the previous October. The rematch was set to take place in Madison Square Garden. This time, Monte got the best of Braddock, keeping Braddock's powerful right hand at bay with a stiff jab. When Braddock connected, it wasn't with the same ferocity and strength that he had in fights prior to the hand injury. Monte earned a decision, and Braddock had his first loss as a pro.

The loss wasn't totally devastating, as it didn't hurt Braddock's standing as a top light-heavyweight contender. *The Ring* still considered Braddock the No. 1 contender to champion Tommy Loughran. The loss might have been a temporary hindrance, but it was nothing that Braddock couldn't handle. It was just the first obstacle in what would become a career of setbacks.

Braddock recovered in time to win a 10-round decision over Nando Tassi in a Madison Square Garden undercard on July 25, 1928, and then he took on a highly regarded light-heavyweight from Ohio named Joe Sekyra. A year later, Sekyra would climb into the ring against a German fighter named Max Schmeling.

Earlier that year, Sekyra had battled Loughran to a 10-round no-decision in Louisville, so he was clearly a formidable foe for Braddock. On August 8, 1928, Sekyra had his way with Braddock, taking a 10-round decision. The big Irishman had been defeated for the second time in three bouts, after thirty-eight fights without a loss. Some sceptics and detractors now questioned whether Braddock really had the goods to be a contender. He was going to have to prove himself worthy, and in a hurry. That credibility came in Braddock's very next fight.

# 4

fter the loss to Joe Sekyra, Braddock's manager
Joe Gould wanted to find another quality
opponent right away. He wanted to seize the
opportunity before Braddock's reputation suffered any
further damage. So Gould arranged a fight with Pete
Latzo, a hard-nosed, never-say-die Slavic fighter who
had defeated Mickey Walker, one of Braddock's heroes,
to win the welterweight championship of the world in
Scranton, Pennsylvania, in May of 1926. Latzo had held
that title for a little more than a year.

Latzo had also faced Tommy Loughran twice in
1928, on June 1 and again on July 16, both times with
Loughran's light-heavyweight title on the line. Latzo,

who had moved up in weight class from welterweight to light-heavy, couldn't handle Loughran's speed and agility and dropped both title bouts, both by decision, one in 15 rounds, the other in 10.

Gould figured that a bout with Latzo would be good for his fighter, and he was right. On October 17, 1928, Braddock entered the ring in a Newark hotel ballroom as a 2-to-1 underdog, even though he had a good seven–inch height advantage over Latzo.

But early in the fight, Braddock's monstrous right hand magically reappeared—with the same intensity and strength that he had possessed during his undefeated run. One overhand right shattered Latzo's jaw, and although Latzo managed to finish the fight, Braddock had an impressive 10-round decision. Another loss would have been devastating to Braddock's ascent in the light-heavyweight ranks, but an impressive win over a proven champion like Latzo kept Gould's plans of turning Braddock into a champion intact.

The victory set up a headlining event at Madison Square Garden, with Braddock pitted against Harold "Tuffy" Griffiths, a burly light-heavyweight from Sioux City, Iowa who came into the fight with a huge reputation and an undefeated record.

Some sportswriters who followed Griffiths into town for the November 30 fight reported that the fighter came to Madison Square Garden with a 56-0 record, but in reality, it was more like 36-0 with 22 knockouts. Still, Braddock was an underdog once again, going up against a brawler with an undefeated record and a solid reputation as perhaps the biggest challenger to Loughran.

"Tuffy Griffiths came from out West and he was licking all the light-heavyweights," Braddock told Heller. "They brought him in and matched him with me."

As it turned out, it was a mismatch. Griffiths couldn't withstand the strength and power of Braddock. The hometown hero made everyone in the Garden happy again with a second-round knockout, a devastation of mammoth proportions. Braddock was now all the way back, and on track for a title shot.

"It was a tremendous boost for me," Braddock told Heller.

It was a great way for Braddock to finish 1928. He was getting good purses, around $15,000 per fight. He was financially well off, and still investing wisely with the help of some close friends and advisors. He even put some of his purses into local savings-and-loans. Braddock also met a beautiful brunette by the name of Mae Fox, a woman with whom he would eventually spend the rest of his life.

It wasn't hard to fall for Mae Fox. She was gorgeous, intelligent and extremely loyal. She loved her big burly man and was willing to accept everything about Jimmy Braddock's life, including his boxing career, which was at its highest point after the big win over Griffiths.

As 1929 began, Braddock was featured on the cover of *The Ring*. He was also slated to fight another tough light-heavyweight named Leo Lomski, also a much heavier fighter than Braddock, on January 18. Known as "The Aberdeen Assassin," because he moved to Aberdeen, Washington after starting his pro boxing career, Lomski had reached almost folk-hero status in the Northwest because of his wild and carefree lifestyle (he had been a lumberjack and log roller in Idaho). His career met the same eventual fate as those of several other Braddock foes: a loss to Tommy Loughran in a bid for the light-heavyweight crown. Lomski fell to Loughran in 1928, although to his credit, he did knock the seemingly impenetrable Loughran to the canvas.

But Lomski had wins over Pete Latzo and Joe Sekyra in the same year, which gave him major credibility, and he'd also beaten Braddock's friend, Jimmy Francis, and the future light-heavyweight champion and Hall of Famer Maxie Rosenbloom. Lomski had a solid reputation; he was also Jewish, which was an oddity for a fighter from the Great Northwest.

"My brother and me were the only Jewish boys in the whole city of Aberdeen," Lomski told a reporter before the fight against Braddock.

Braddock thought he had a good chance against Lomski. So did Gould. The Braddock camp was brimming with confidence going into the fight. More than 18,000 fans packed the Garden, and a total purse of over $65,000 was collected. Unfortunately, Lomski was given a 10-round decision over Braddock, whose record dropped to 30-3. He did still walk away with a payday of approximately $20,000.

It was yet another setback in Braddock's professional life, but as he had proven before, he had the ability to bounce back; in fact, he would almost reinvent himself after the ups and downs of the prior six months. There had been three tough losses, to Monte, Sekyra and now Lomski. But there had also been impressive wins over Latso and Griffiths.

Braddock's professional career wasn't in jeopardy after the loss to Lomski, but he was going to need another big win to get back to top-contender status.

On February 4, 1929, Braddock climbed back into the ring against George Gemas in Newark, in the same venue where he had pummeled Latzo's jaw. A strong local following was in attendance as Braddock destroyed Gemas with a straight right and knocked him out in the first round. He was the Jimmy Braddock of old, scoring a first-round knockout in the same fashion as he had three years earlier when his professional career had begun.

The impressive dismantling of Gemas sent the message that the up-and-down Braddock was indeed back. It was enough for Madison Square Garden promoters to bring the local hero to New York for another headliner, this time against former light-heavyweight champion Jimmy Slattery.

Slattery, who had held the title in 1927 only to relinquish it to Tommy Loughran, was the favourite hero of

Buffalo, New York. Another Irish fighter, he was known in his hometown as "Jimmy Slats with the savage right clip."

Unlike Braddock, who was conscientious about his earnings, Slattery was a fun-loving spendthrift who apparently felt free to give his fortune, estimated at more than $450,000 over his professional career, away to anyone and everyone. One time, a group of 28 friends from Buffalo traveled to New York City to see Slattery fight at the Garden. The entire group showed up at Slattery's hotel after the fight, but they informed the champ that they had spent all their money and had no way of getting home. No problem, Jimmy Slats said. He got on the phone and bought 28 Pullman train tickets to Buffalo.

Slattery told friends and reporters that he would give up boxing in a heartbeat if he could make a living playing the piano or the harmonica. In fact, Slattery was known to play the harmonica to loosen up right before fights.

There were stories of Slattery simply dropping out of sight for days on end. Slattery's manager, an old boxing curmudgeon named Red Carr, once set up a match for Slattery that would have been a good stepping stone toward a contending fight. But Slattery disappeared and could not be found. Five days later, Carr received a Western Union telegram stating that Slattery had been arrested in Elkhart, Indiana for public intoxication and vagrancy.

He disappeared again in Venice, Italy. After four days, his entourage contacted Venice police, who prepared to dredge the canals in search of a body; the only way out of

Venice at the time was by boat, and Slattery wasn't on any passenger list. At 4 a.m., just before the police started to search the waters, Slattery was spotted, drifting in on a purloined gondola, sound asleep.

But Slattery was a favourite of fight fans and experts. Gentleman Jim Corbett went to every Slattery fight and predicted he would become the next heavyweight champion of the world. Sportswriters reported that Corbett said he saw a lot of himself in Slattery. Gene Tunney, the heavyweight champion at the time, called Slattery "the greatest natural boxer of the time."

However, Slattery's fondness for alcohol, women and song prevented him from maintaining his greatness.

When Braddock signed on to fight Slattery, he was once again an underdog, facing a former champion, and with a considerable weight disadvantage. Bookmakers outside the Garden on March 11, 1929 had Slattery as almost a 2-to-1 favourite.

"I was always more or less the underdog," Braddock said in the Heller book. "But it didn't make no difference to me."

Obviously not. Braddock and Slattery engaged in an all-out war, one of the most physical bouts of Jimmy Braddock's career. The two men were proud warriors, and they gave all that they had.

But Braddock finally prevailed in a ninth-round technical knockout that pushed his career record to 32-3 and catapulted him to the top of the contender's list in the light-heavyweight class.

On April 22, Braddock traveled to Slattery's native Buffalo and took on another up-and-comer, Eddie Benson, who was disposed of in typical Braddock fashion with a first-round knockout.

Now Braddock was ready for the big time. Gould was busy securing Braddock his first title shot. Tommy Loughran awaited.

# 5

As the summer of 1929 kicked into full gear, Joe Gould challenged Philadelphia native Tommy Loughran to defend his light-heavyweight championship against Jimmy Braddock. The Loughran camp, led by the shrewd veteran manager Joe Smith, accepted the challenge.

Loughran was the best there was. Although he didn't possess a big knockout punch—he'd won only 17 bouts by knockout in a career of 172 fights—Loughran was considered by some experts to be the most skilled fighter in the history of the light-heavyweight division and perhaps the entire sport.

Loughran was from the old school of boxing, leading with a reaching right-hand jab and finishing with a strong and efficient left. Loughran's left had become famous because of the accuracy and the timing with which he threw it; it was a style of punch in direct contrast to the blunt power of Braddock's booming right.

While most boxers of that era concentrated on power and delivering a knockout punch, Loughran was more of a surgeon in the ring, a tactician who concentrated on every precise move. For example, Loughran had a habit of ending each round near his corner, so he would be able to sit and catch more rest, while his opponent had to walk across the ring to take his seat.

Ironically, Loughran had become proficient with his left hand because he'd suffered a severely broken right hand in a fight and had to continue his career with a change in strategy.

"I was never sure if the right hand would ever hold up the same way ever again," Loughran said in an interview about his change of style. "I had to be able to do something. I had a bad right hand all throughout my career. That, and not any weak hitting on my part, was the real reason why I had to rely upon my left."

The general fight fan found Loughran's style somewhat boring: if you went to a Loughran fight, you were almost sure not to see a knockout. He wasn't going to put anyone away, but he wasn't going to get knocked out himself either. He had a very tough jaw to back up his tactics.

The fight fan of the 1920s usually came to the smoky arenas and bingo halls with one thing in mind: to see a knockout. That's why brawlers like Jimmy Braddock were more popular than the reigning champion.

However, boxing purists were amazed at Loughran's skill. Gentleman Jim Corbett once said that Loughran "does things in the ring that I always wanted to do." They were impressed with his master footwork and strategy, especially his ability to control the pace and direction of each round so he could finish in his own corner every time.

In 1922, Loughran had fought the heavyweight champ Gene Tunney to a no-decision in Loughran's native Philadelphia. In fact, in a time when no-decisions were more prevalent, Loughran once fought a stretch of 22 bouts with a winner declared in only three of the matches. A lot of the reason for this was that judges weren't sold on Loughran's style.

However, Tunney came away impressed. "Lacking a punch, the strongest and best natural defense in boxing, Loughran did more with what he had than any fighter in my experience," Tunney said after the fight.

One fight that did come to a decision in Loughran's career was his January 30, 1923 bout against Harry Greb, a boxer who Loughran would face six times in his Hall of Fame career. This time, Greb was the light-heavyweight champion and he defeated Loughran in a 15-round decision, although Loughran believed he had won the fight.

"I had boxed Greb twice before in no-decision bouts, but I soon found out that Harry was an entirely different proposition with a decision on the line," Loughran said. "I never saw so many gloves in all my life. Fighting Greb was a boxing education. All styles were simple to me after I met Greb."

It took four full years of action before Loughran would get a chance at the light-heavyweight title. In 1926, he fought and defeated Georges Carpentier, the French fighter who had battled with Jack Dempsey in a heavyweight title bout in 1921. The Loughran-Carpentier fight took place at Boyle's Thirty Acres in Jersey City and drew more than 100,000 fans to see the sport's first $1 million purse. In October, 1927, Loughran defeated Mike McTigue in Madison Square Garden to capture the light-heavyweight title in a 15-round decision, and then two months later he picked apart former champ Jimmy Slattery to earn the National Boxing Association light-heavyweight belt as well.

Over the next two years, Loughran won 10 straight bouts, all via decisions, defending his title four times against great fighters like Leo Lomski (January 6, 1928), Pete Latzo twice (June 1 and July 16, 1928) and the famed Mickey Walker, who Braddock admired and styled himself after. Walker, the former welterweight and middleweight champion of the world, lost a 10-round decision to Loughran in Chicago on March 28, 1929, in a fight that reportedly had a shady side.

In a strange deal, Walker, who went by the nickname "The Toy Bulldog," was promised $10,000 if he defeated Loughran for the title, but $50,000 if he lost the fight. The strange setup was put together as a financial security blanket for Walker, who was the middleweight champ at the time but was taking a huge risk by stepping up into the world of the light-heavies.

After losing to Loughran, Walker twice defeated Leo Lomski and held on to the middleweight championship until 1931, when he relinquished it in search of bigger paydays.

Loughran was clearly the king of the light-heavyweight class, and again Braddock was the underdog, this time at 8-to-5. The fight was scheduled for Yankee Stadium on July 18, 1929. A crowd in excess of 45,000 was expected, so that meant a solid purse, maybe reaching $500,000. Win or lose, Braddock was going to be financially set. Or so it seemed. He was guaranteed at least $30,000 for the Loughran fight.

"After just three years, I figured it was a hell of an honour to fight for the championship, as far as I was concerned," Braddock told Heller.

In the opening minute of the fight, Braddock unleashed his powerful right hand, and it seemed enough to produce a typical first-round knockout. A huge cut opened up over Loughran's left eye, making it tough for the champion to see. It appeared that Braddock was about to claim his first championship belt.

But the cut just seemed to invigorate the southpaw Loughran. In fact, with his footwork in place and his tactical genius in gear, the Philly fighter was barely touched again for the course of the 15 rounds. Loughran used his left to outpoint Braddock in every conceivable fashion. Throughout the fight, Braddock appeared to be frustrated by Loughran's elusiveness and inability to get hurt by anything except that first-round punch.

As it turned out, it was the most one-sided defeat in Braddock's career. He didn't even come close. The official scoring was never reported, but everyone in attendance knew who the champion was. One Philadelphia sportswriter reported that Loughran simply "vanished from punches" in that fight, and gave Loughran the nickname "The Phantom of Philly."

"I knew Tommy Loughran was a good boxer," Braddock said after the fight. "I was more or less a boxer-puncher. I figured that I had to try to fight Tommy, not box him. Because, as far as boxing goes, I know I was outclassed beforehand and I was. He beat me in fifteen rounds so easy with his boxing ability. He was a guy you could never hit with a good solid punch."

Still, Braddock had his biggest payday to date, and it was only one loss. He was still very young, having just turned 23. He still had an impressive record of 33-4. He made plans to marry Mae. There was enough money in the bank, and the rest was tied up in good, solid stock investments. He wasn't one to squander his wealth like Jimmy Slattery did; Jimmy Braddock knew he wanted to be a good family man and a good provider. He had no idea just how tough the future was going to become.

# 6

**J**im Braddock thought the loss to Tommy Loughran took something out of him. He admitted as much later on, but he already knew it in his heart after the fight. Something had changed. His mighty right hand, already broken once, was causing some constant pain. Joe Gould thought that it might be better for Braddock to start to think about the heavyweight field; that as long as Loughran was ruling the light-heavyweight world, there was no chance there.

So Braddock began to put on some weight, which meant it would be difficult to go back to the light-heavyweight class. Still, Gould figured the change would be the best thing for Braddock's career. Although the loss to Loughran was a tough one, it wasn't the end of the world. There would be other fights, other challenges. Gould figured that his fighter had come back and defeated the odds a few times before, so he could bounce back once again, even after the lopsided loss.

Gould wanted to get Braddock back into the ring quickly, perhaps to get the taste of the loss to Loughran out of his mouth. So he set up a heavyweight undercard bout against Yale Okun, a perennial challenger from New York who had lost to the likes of Tommy Loughran (twice), Harry Greb and John Henry Lewis.

While Okun was certainly no pushover and provided a good challenge to Braddock, he was not expected to win the fight. But Okun managed to jab and punch his way to a 10-round-decision victory. It marked the first time in Braddock's career that he had dropped two straight bouts. A lot of sceptics started to doubt Braddock's physical ability. Some even questioned his heart, which no one had ever dared to doubt before. They might have questioned his talent and wondered whether he was over his head in some of his more recent fights, but no one had ever thought Braddock was losing his desire to be in the ring.

Soon after the Okun loss, Braddock suffered another huge setback, as did most of the country. The stock-market crash occurred in October of 1929, sending the United States spiraling toward the Great Depression.

No one could have ever predicted the financial devastation that the crash would cause. It was totally unforeseen.

Since the turn of the century, most of the financial activity that took place in the United States centered around the New York Stock Exchange. Owners of big corporations put shares of stock in their respective companies on sale to the general public, with each share of stock representing a proportionate share of that corporation.

In the 1920s, the New York Stock Exchange experienced an unprecedented boom. From 1920 to 1929, stocks more than quadrupled in value. Since Braddock had invested a lot of his purse money in an assortment of stocks, he had watched his personal portfolio do very well. Like Braddock, many other investors became convinced that stocks were a sure thing and invested heavily in the market.

But in October, 1929, the stock prices started to plummet at a rate never seen before, almost falling off the proverbial cliff. Braddock watched his carefully nurtured nest egg start to dwindle.

The stock-market crash had other drastic effects on the economy. The general demand for goods declined, because the public believed they were poor after their huge losses in the stock market. No new investment in the business world could be financed through the sale of stock, because no one would buy the new stock.

Perhaps most important was the trickle-down effect that the crash had on the banking industry, as banks and savings-and-loans tried to collect on loans made to stock-market investors whose holdings were now worth little or nothing.

Even worse, many of the lending institutions had themselves invested depositors' money in the stock market, naturally thinking it a sure thing like the rest of the general public did. When word went out that banks' assets contained huge uncollectable loans and almost-worthless stock certificates, depositors rushed to withdraw their savings. Unable to raise fresh funds from the Federal Reserve system, banks began to fail by the hundreds.

It has never been reported just how much money Jim Braddock lost in the crash of 1929, but it is estimated to be about $300,000, maybe more. There are no official records of how much Braddock invested in stocks and how much he put into the bank.

Losing the money became a very touchy subject to Braddock; to his dying day he never liked to talk about it. Braddock fit the Irish image to a tee: stubborn, unrelenting and proud. He never even discussed the financial situation with his manager Gould, who knew how much his fighter had earned and who also took a financial beating.

Even his fiancée may not have realized just how devastating a loss it was to her future husband. Still, they were married the next year and began a life together, and they would eventually have three children.

Even in his biography, all Braddock says is that "we had it tough for a while."

Yet times were about to get tougher. On November 15,

1929, Braddock was paired against Maxie Rosenbloom, known affectionately in the boxing game as "Slapsie Maxie."

Rosenbloom was a colourful character who was born in Leonard's Bridge, Connecticut, but lived most of his life in New York. He was a strategic boxer, very crafty, hard to hit with a power punch. He didn't possess a devastating punch of his own and appeared at times to hit opponents with the palm portion of the open glove; hence his nickname.

Coincidentally, it was Damon Runyon who first called Rosenbloom "Slapsie Maxie" and who would later give Braddock his own famous nickname.

Rosenbloom was the busiest boxer in the history of the sport. As a professional, he entered the ring almost 300 times over a 16-year career. Of those fights, Rosenbloom won 210 and lost just 38. (26 bouts ended in draws and another 23 were no-decisions.) But—proving how much of a slap boxer he truly was—he had only 19 career knockouts.

Rosenbloom loved to kid boxing judges because they didn't know how to score his fights. He received so many draws that he once said, "If I win, can I get a draw, too?" It was a line that stayed with Rosenbloom throughout his career.

Rosenbloom was also an equal-opportunity fighter. In an era when many of the top fighters tended to shy away from facing African-Americans, Rosenbloom made a living from facing black fighters. Over his career, 70 of his fights were against black boxers—a far greater number than any other white fighter of the era had taken on.

The legend has it that Rosenbloom moved to Harlem with his family when he was just a toddler, quit school after "t'ird" grade and ended up in a reform school. He once told reporters that he had to "quit school in da t'ird grade, because I didn't wanna pass my fadder, who was in da fourt'."

Apparently, while attending that reform school, it was the actor and legendary tough guy George Raft of the original *Scarface* who spotted the young Rosenbloom in a street brawl and suggested that he become a boxer.

Rosenbloom went professional at 19 and quickly began a rigorous schedule, fighting as often as 25 times a year.

"Slapsie Maxie," who claimed he never took a drink in his life, maintained a whirlwind boxing schedule and an even more tiring lifestyle. He was known to be the last one to leave dancehalls and restaurants, in order to be around women. In the ring, Rosenbloom seemed to always be having a good time, laughing and infuriating his opponents with his slap-happy approach. He once said, "I didn't want to hurt nobody. I just smack them around and let them know who was boss."

During one stretch before his showdown with Braddock, Rosenbloom fought an amazing four times in 13 days, from August 16 to 29, including bouts against Harry Martone (in Bayonne, New Jersey) and "Cuban" Bobby Brown (in Franklin, New Jersey) on successive nights.

Rosenbloom won both bouts in 10-round decisions. Just before he was slated to take on Braddock on Noember15, 1929 in Madison Square Garden, Rosenbloom also had consecutive wins over Jimmy Slattery, whom Braddock had defeated, and Joe Sekyra, who had defeated Braddock.

Again, a sloppy and sluggish Braddock took it on the chin, as "Slapsie Maxie" slapped his way to a 10-round-decision win. It was Braddock's third straight loss. His record now stood at 33-6. His career as a contender was slipping away. He needed a break.

So, before the end of the year, Gould arranged a preliminary-card fight against Jake Warren in Brooklyn. Braddock showed a glimmer of hope on the December 7 bout, knocking out Warren in the second round for his first win in eight months.

But nothing would save Braddock from his financial woes. He tried his best to keep it to himself, but the money that he thought he'd tucked safely away to save for Mae and a rainy day down the road was long gone.

*Braddock and his wife Mae smile as they watch a exhibition arranged by New York State Troopers, Sidney, New York, June 4, 1935. Braddock wears a state trooper's hat. (Photo by FPG/Getty Images)*

# 7

"Slapsie Maxie" Rosenbloom was able to use the victory over Jimmy Braddock as a stepping stone to future fights. Even though he had about 85 professional fights before defeating Braddock at the Garden and receiving a nice payday, the win set him up to move on in the light-heavyweight ranks.

Rosenbloom first defeated Leo Lomski in January of 1930, then he beat Jimmy Slattery—in Buffalo, of all places—on June 25, 1930 to win the light-heavyweight championship of the world (Loughran relinquished the title in September of 1929), a title that he would hold for four and a half years, fighting an incomprehensible 106 times during that stretch. He finally lost the title to Bob Olin via decision in November of 1934.

Rosenbloom later became a popular entertainer in movies, on radio, in night clubs, and much later, on television. He appeared in more than 100 movies after his retirement from the ring. He never had to concern himself with finding his next payday.

That wasn't the case for Jim Braddock, who now had to worry about finances, like most of the United States. He was also watching his boxing career deteriorate.

As 1930 began, Braddock signed on to fight familiar foe Leo Lomski in Chicago. Struggling and plodding along, Braddock fought Lomski in a 10-round bout and put him on the canvas twice, but the fight was called a draw by the judges. Then, two weeks later, the Illinois State Athletic Commission reversed the judges' decision and declared Lomski the winner. The ridiculous action was known in boxing circles as "The Eleven Day Decision," because that's how long after the fight the ruling came down. It seemed as if Braddock just couldn't catch a single break.

It was Braddock's fourth loss in five bouts and his eighth loss over the last 15. Just two years earlier, Braddock had been an undefeated rising star. Now, still only 23, he was holding on to his career for dear life.

There was some good news to report on the home front. Mae Braddock gave birth to the family's first child, James J. Jr., known affectionately as Jay. Another—son, Howard, and a daughter, Rose Marie, would follow. Braddock was a good family man and cared about his children more than anything. He also adored his wife and didn't want to do anything that would jeopardize their love.

Other professional athletes, especially boxers, had earned reputations as booze hounds, philanderers and cheats. Not Jim Braddock. He came from a good family and wanted to make sure that he gave his own children a good family life as well.

On April 7, 1930, Braddock took to the ring again, this time in Philadelphia. With the man who had started Braddock's decline, Tommy Loughran, in attendance, he tried valiantly to muster some life against a journeyman named Billy Jones. But once again Braddock struggled. He never hurt Jones and took another hard 10-round decision loss, making it five losses in six bouts.

The injuries were now beginning to mount along with the losses. Braddock's right hand never fully healed after the Loughran fight. He was in constant pain. Some doctors said that he had developed "puncher's arthritis," and he had yet to turn 24. He had also suffered broken ribs that had not been properly diagnosed, nor treated. His nose had been broken several times and was constantly running.

Still, fighting was Jim Braddock's lone source of income in June of 1930. As bad as he felt physically, he had to continue to box. He took a fight in his backyard of West New York against Harold Mays on June 5, 1930 and fought 10-rounds to a no-decision. Out-of-town reporters wrote that Mays more than likely won the fight, but that the promoters gave the hometown hero a break and called it a no-decision, so the two could split the prize money, instead of a winner earning more. But the money wasn't near the $10,000 or $15,000 paydays Braddock used to get. The Mays fight earned him about $1,500.

Always looking for a way to promote his fighter, Gould found interest in Boston, with its large Irish population. Braddock got a third crack at the tough Joe Monte, who he'd defeated in 1927, but who then had handed him his first professional defeat in 1928. Almost two years to the day after that first loss, Braddock would have a chance at revenge, although Monte was still considered a contender at the time and Braddock had fallen far off the challenger's rankings in *The Ring* magazine.

Even with the city of Boston in bad financial straits because of the Great Depression, Gould was certain the fight could draw, even with modest ticket prices, if an Irish hero like Braddock was on the card.

As it happened, the turnout for the outdoor venue was sparse. Again, there were some flashes of brilliance, some moments to remember the Braddock of old. He hit his opponent with a series of solid right hands and put the usually impenetrable Monte to the canvas once.

The knockdown was good enough to secure Braddock a 10-round decision—yet another comeback for the King of Comebacks—and one that Gould and Braddock really needed. They were both close to broke.

The same promoters gave Braddock another shot in Boston, hoping to capitalize on any momentum from the Monte fight. They matched him against Alvin "Babe" Hunt, a journeyman heavyweight who a year later would be part of the Jack Dempsey barnstorming exhibition tour.

It was believed that Hunt would be cannon fodder for the experienced Braddock, but Hunt managed to secure a 10-round decision, pushing Braddock's record over the last two years to a less-than formidable 8-10. Braddock did manage to knock out Phil Mercurio, again at an outdoor facility in Boston, on September 19, 1930, in the second round, and then didn't fight for the remainder of the year: there were no other calls from promoters. No chances to earn money in the ring. With a wife and a small child at home, Braddock had to do something to earn more.

He tried his hand as a bartender and as a general labourer. The pay wasn't enough, so he headed back to the Hoboken docks. It seemed unthinkable that a talented athlete who had been one bout away from the light-heavyweight championship of the world would have to return to manual labour.

Gould stuck by his man's side. From the moment he'd spotted Braddock, the manager had never once asked Braddock to sign an official contract. Just a simple handshake bonded the two men forever. Gould vowed he would stick by his protégé through thick and thin. Braddock always loved Gould's loyalty.

As 1931 began, Braddock found himself in a very new predicament: no one wanted to take a chance on him. He wasn't a hot commodity. Any hint of a fight came via the persistence and perseverance of Gould.

Gould managed to get Braddock on a card at the Garden to battle a 215-pound Bull Moose named Ernie Schaaf, who hailed from Elizabeth, New Jersey, the hometown of Braddock's hero Mickey Walker.

On January 23, 1931, Schaaf overpowered Braddock, sending him to a painful defeat via a 10-round decision. It was not a pretty sight. Obviously favouring his injured hand, Braddock tried to stay with the heavier Schaaf to no avail. Braddock suffered his seventh loss in 11 fights against three wins and one no-decision.

Almost two years later, on February 10, 1933, Schaaf would fight the mammoth Italian Primo Carnera in a heavyweight contending fight. It was a brutal mismatch: the 6'7", 285-pound Carnera knocked out Schaaf in the 13th round. Two days later, Schaaf died of the injuries he had suffered in the fight. He was 24 years old.

Once again, Braddock was down in the dumps. The losses were piling up, and so were the bills. It was beyond a trying time for Jim Braddock and his new bride. Once again, Braddock was going to have to find some inner strength to muster yet another comeback. He had to prove to promoters that he was still a viable contender, a worthy draw. It wasn't going to be easy.

**8**

After Braddock's loss to Schaaf, Gould figured that his fighter needed some confidence-building. Braddock had lost 11 of his last 21 bouts and was a mere shell of the fighter who'd taken on Tommy Loughran for the light-heavy title just two years earlier.

Since losing to Loughran, Braddock had climbed into the ring 10 times. He had three wins, with only the decision over old foe Joe Monte considered a good victory. He had six losses, some of which were understandable, like to the tough Leo Lomski and the much bigger Ernie Schaaf, but some of which were downright horrible. And, he had the one no-decision, against Harold Mays, which could have been a loss if the hometown judges hadn't given him a break.

Gould found Braddock a couple of pushovers. The paydays were trivial, less than $1,000 each. But they were paydays nonetheless, which meant that Braddock was going to be able to provide some semblance of a living for his wife and burgeoning family.

Braddock hopped a train to Miami for a fight on March 5, 1931, to take on a heavyweight by the name of Jack Roper, who also fought under the name of Clifford Byron Hammond. The fighter's hometown was Hollywood, California, and with a pseudonym like Clifford Byron Hammond, maybe he was better suited for motion pictures than a boxing ring.

Roper entered the ring for the fight with a record that was even more troubling than Braddock's. He had lost 12 straight times and was earning a reputation as a card-filling pushover. Roper's less-than-stellar career would end with a record of 53-43-10, certainly not the stuff that champions are made of. It was not going to be a memorable bout. Braddock dispensed with Roper in what used to be a traditional first-round knockout.

Later that month, Gould found another pushover waiting in New Haven, Connecticut, again as part of a very low-level boxing card. This time the opponent was a Connecticut heavyweight named Jack Kelly, who was in even more dire straits than Roper/Hammond.

Kelly was what boxing experts called a "bum," a guy who would simply climb into the ring and get his head handed to him for a small fee. It was a tag that Braddock himself was trying hard not to acquire.

Once you were labeled a bum in the boxing game, there was generally no hope for recovery. The bum was the guy who entered the ring with a torn robe, too poor to hire a manager, trainer or cut man. The bums in boxing were loners, but they had a place in the game because they were good cannon fodder for the up-and-coming contenders.

The bums were also somewhat appealing to the promoters, who wanted to fill out multi-bout cards and needed to find warm bodies.

Jimmy Braddock never wanted to see the day when he, a once-promising contender was labeled a mere purse-hungry bum, like Jack Kelly.

Kelly entered the ring with a 7-9 career record, but he gave Braddock everything he could handle. Braddock won a tough 10-round decision in a fight in which the two Irishmen gave the crowd more than they could have wanted for their $1 admission. Braddock took his $1,000 purse and headed home to West New York and to Mae and Jay, Jr., a beaten and tired soul. He was in pain. His hands were getting worse and worse, especially the once-mighty right hand.

But there was no time to waste. Bills had to be paid. A few days after Braddock returned home from Connecticut, he went back to the docks of Hoboken to work, hurting from head to toe.

Needing money, Gould worked feverishly to find Braddock more work in the ring. But no one seemed to be impressed with his fighter's two wins over Roper and Kelly. The well had seemingly run dry.

Even though he was struggling financially, Braddock decided to step away from the ring for a little while. Maybe his hands would heal with good rest. Maybe the assorted aches and pains would go away. Gould worked on finding remedies for Braddock's puncher's arthritis.

Between March and September of 1931, Braddock did not box. He continued to be a good provider for his family. He worked hard at the docks while the country continued to plunge further and further into the Great Depression.

But while Americans were feeling bad about their financial plight, sports provided an excellent outlet. Baseball was the national pastime and the New York Yankees were the dominant draw, with Babe Ruth and Lou Gehrig leading the way. Nothing could diminish the mystique of baseball, even in the 1930s. It was solidly entrenched in the hearts and minds of all Americans, regardless of the financial ruin.

At the same time, thoroughbred horse racing was just beginning its ascent into the American mainstream. It saw such incredible growth that it would quickly become the most heavily attended sport in America. Pari-mutuel racing, banned in many states for decades, was being reinstituted in places like California as a way to try to give the economy a jump-start.

But boxing always had its special place with the poor and the aristocracy alike. Boxing provided heroes for the everyman. The Irish had Jim Corbett to admire. The Jewish kids could look to someone like "Slapsie Maxie" Rosenbloom as one of their own.

And then there was Jack Dempsey, the "Manassas Mauler," who had retired from boxing in 1927 after his controversial loss to Gene Tunney before 104,000 fans in Soldier Field in Chicago, but who was still such a popular athlete in America that he embarked on a "comeback" tour in 1931, traveling the country and performing in boxing exhibitions.

Dempsey was considering a comeback to competitive boxing and figured that he could capitalize on his immense popularity with the tour, which went mostly through America's Heartland and the Great Northwest. He fought in an amazing 73 exhibitions (mostly one- and two-round affairs) in 1931 alone, in places like Portland, Seattle, and Spokane. On one September day in Boise, Dempsey fought five different opponents, each man getting one round to go toe-to-toe with the great champ. Barnstorming tours became a way of life for popular athletes and entertainers alike during the Great Depression.

Braddock especially admired Dempsey, and in later life the two became very close friends.

Those were the three sports of the Great Depression—baseball, horse racing and boxing. They dominated the sports pages of the newspapers and filled the newswires in the cinemas.

While Dempsey was touring the country, taking advantage of his popularity and his drawing power, Jim

Braddock was slaving away, trying to make a decent living on the docks. Boxing was almost becoming an afterthought, because the sport was somehow staying away from Braddock.

Then Gould received a wire in late August of 1931. Braddock was wanted for a fight in Detroit against Andy Mitchell, a Kansas-born and California-bred heavyweight with a less-than-stellar résumé, but who was trained by Jack "Doc" Kearns, the manager/trainer of Mickey Walker.

Kearns was looking for a solid opponent for Mitchell and he quickly thought of Braddock. Gould gladly accepted the challenge. The respite was over.

On September 3, 1931, Braddock took on Mitchell and proved right away that the layoff had done him some good. He was fresh, on his toes and showed some pop in his punches, although he was still not the same fighter he'd been four years earlier. Braddock hurt Mitchell early in the fight and then won a lopsided 10-round decision. It was his third straight victory. Maybe there was some light at the end of the tunnel after all, Gould thought. Maybe this kid has yet another comeback in him.

# 9

After first gaining a reputation as a light-heavyweight contender, then losing a lot of credibility with his descent in the ranks, maybe Jim Braddock was reinventing himself as the autumn of 1931 arrived.

With three straight victories, Braddock was once again on the climb. He was giving "roller coaster career" a new meaning. Braddock had some confidence, even if the three opponents had been nothing to write home about, they were three wins all the same.

Joe Gould, always thinking, wanted to push the idea that Braddock was the quintessential underdog. Maybe he could catch lightning in a bottle: build some momentum and popularity, reestablish his fighter as a legitimate opponent and possible contender.

Gould also thought that if the public bought into the "comeback kid" idea, it might lead to more bouts and better purses, which were definitely what Gould and Braddock needed if they wanted to survive in the fight game. Because by the fall of 1931, the Great Depression was tightening its stranglehold on the nation. Hundreds of thousands of Americans were living below poverty level, wondering where they next dollar would come from, where they would get their next meal.

While Braddock wasn't exactly starving just yet, he wasn't rich either. He continued to look for steady work at the Hoboken docks when he wasn't in the ring. He also took a few turns as a bartender in local gin mills. At least, when he was bartending, Braddock was giving his body some time to heal.

With the momentum carrying, Gould signed Braddock up for another fight against a formidable opponent, and one with whom he was familiar: Joe Sekrya.

At one time, the Berwick, Pennsylvania-born and Dayton, Ohio-raised Sekrya had been a solid contender for the heavyweight title, but in 1930 and 1931, he had fallen on tough times like Braddock and had lost more than he won. Sekrya was being used as ring fodder for the up-and-comers now, trying hard to hang on to his career.

But Sekrya had once handled Braddock, giving him his second professional loss. Although that fight had been only three years earlier it now seemed like eons ago, considering the path that both boxers' lives and careers had taken.

Braddock and Sekrya met in a 10-round undercard bout in a six-bout fight night at Madison Square Garden on October 9, 1931, and the result was not good for the local hero. Once again, Sekrya got the best of Braddock and won a well-earned 10-round decision.

In later years, both fighters would say that the war between the two on that October date in 1931 took a lot out of them for the remainders of their careers.

Sekrya was never the same fighter again. For the final six years of his career, Sekrya became a journeyman, a "bum," a card-filler who bounced from ring to ring. He ended his career in 1937 with a very average 48-34-4 career record.

A month later, Braddock took on another familiar foe, namely "Slapsie Maxie" Rosenbloom, in a heavyweight fight in Minneapolis. But after two rounds, the fight was ruled a no-contest by referee George Barton.

Word had filtered down that there was an apparent prearranged agreement: Rosenbloom would allow Braddock to win in an attempt to get Braddock back on the beam. When Barton received word of the deal, the fight was stopped.

Braddock was supposed to receive $996 for his efforts; Rosenbloom $1,195. The Minnesota Boxing Commission allowed each fighter to keep $350 for training expenses. The rest of the purses were donated to charity.

Less than a month later, Braddock was paired in the main event of a two-bout card in New Haven, Connecticut, against Al Gainer, a formidable former light-heavyweight who was now testing the heavyweight waters. Again, the results weren't positive for Braddock, who lost a 10-round decision, dropping his career record to 38-13.

Although the payday was over $1,000 for Braddock, both he and Gould realized that the chances of getting such purses were rapidly slipping away. It was only going to get worse before it got better.

Back home, Braddock learned that Mae was pregnant with the couple's second child. Now the financial pressures were really beginning to mount. As 1932 began, as the nation fell further into the financial depths, Jimmy Braddock's boxing career was hanging by a thread.

Not even the smaller venues were considering Braddock any longer, which meant that he had to continue to work on the docks for very minimal pay in order to keep his family out of complete financial despair.

Braddock returned to the ring on March 18, 1932, in an undercard at Chicago Stadium, with the main event being the National Boxing Association light-heavyweight title fight between George Nichols and Dave Maier. Braddock was paired against a journeyman light-heavyweight named Baxter Calmes, a mediocre Wichita, Kansas-based fighter who lacked a knockout punch. Calmes had a very average career record of 22-9 with 10 knockouts, but he totally dominated Braddock and earned a 10-round unanimous decision.

The major slide had begun for Braddock. He had lost three straight decisions to journeyman fighters. The transformation was complete. Braddock had become a bum, a body to throw into the ring against the promising contenders.

The one thing that Gould and Braddock had tried hardest to avoid had happened. He was run-of-the-mill, a pushover. No one would ever have thought it was possible when Braddock's career began.

On May 13, 1932, Braddock went to Boston Garden to become cannon fodder for a heavyweight-title contender named Charley Retzlaff, who was born in a small town called Leonard, North Dakota and then made Duluth, Minnesota his home.

"Big Charley R" was a solid 196-pound right-hander who would later fight Joe Louis as Louis made his ascent toward the heavyweight title. He possessed a powerful punch and good knockout ability. He had a 16-pound advantage on Braddock, and he outpointed him in 10 rounds, sending Braddock to defeat for his fourth straight decision, pushing the career record to 38-15.

Braddock began to personally question his ability and started to think that perhaps boxing wasn't for him. But the work at the docks was becoming less and less frequent by the summer of 1932. Sure, Braddock would show up there every day, and more than likely he would be hired. But on more and more days he was turned away, told he wasn't needed. He worked four, then three days per week. So while his boxing career was floundering, the chance to earn regular work and wages was dwindling, too.

Braddock got another fight on June 21, this time as the walk-out bout after the main event, the heavyweight battle between champions Jack Sharkey and Max Schmeling at the Madison Square Garden Bowl in Long Island City, New York, a bout that was for both the National Boxing Association and the New York State Athletic Commission heavyweight crowns.

After Sharkey defeated Schmeling in a controversial 15-round split decision that featured some of the most bizarre scoring in boxing history (Referee Ed "Gunboat" Smith had it 7-3 for Sharkey with five rounds even, Judge George Kelly had it 8-7 for Sharkey, and Judge Charles Mathieson had it 10-5 in favour of Schmeling), the crowd of 55,000 began to filter out of the Garden Bowl.

Into the ring stepped Braddock, with not many people paying much attention, especially since Braddock's opponent was Vincent Parille, a native of Argentina who had grown up in Bloomfield, New Jersey and had somehow acquired an alias of Stanley Ketchell, that he used from time to time. Parille was an unpolished fighter with an unorthodox style and a 10-4 record, but Braddock made the most of his experience advantage and earned a five-round decision.

At the very least, the losing streak was over. The other positive was that Braddock had been part of a heavyweight-championship card, even if his fight had taken place when most of the paying customers were heading for the exits. Yet once again, Braddock had a win that he could possibly build on. What lay ahead was almost too unthinkable for words.

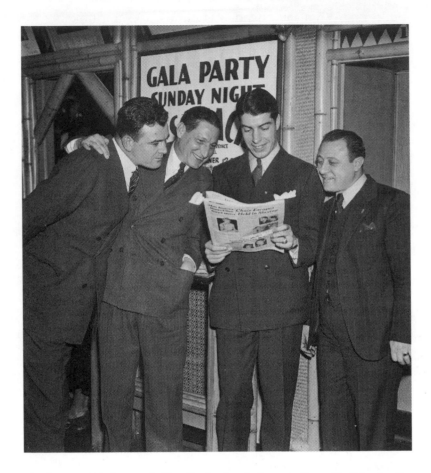

*(Left to right) James J. Braddock, baseball comedian Al Schack, Joe DiMaggio and his friend, Mike Carobreese reading Walter Winchell's "Scoop" story. (Photo © Corbis. All rights reserved.)*

# 10

month after beating Parille in the Garden Bowl, Jim Braddock returned to the venue, this time to take on a promising 22-year-old heavyweight from Boston named Tony Shucco in the middle bout of a three-fight card on July 25, 1932.

Shucco possessed an impressive 41-5 record when he climbed into the ring against Braddock, and he'd recently defeated Max Rosenbloom and Jack Kelly, former Braddock foes.

Braddock had a rare weight advantage (181 to 177), but it didn't help. Shucco won an eight-round decision, which dropped Braddock to 39-16 lifetime.

Joe Gould wasn't able to line up another bout for his

struggling fighter until September. After all, Braddock had gone 12-16 since starting his career with 27 straight victories. Not many promoters were willing to give a fight to a boxer in obvious decline. Braddock's take-home pay for a fight was now about $650 to $750.

Any popularity that Braddock might have gained with the three straight victories a year earlier was long gone. He was looking like a washed-out fighter, a total has-been. Some of his closest friends in boxing, people like Mickey Walker and Jack Dempsey, were trying to convince Braddock that it was time to walk away.

But Braddock was not ready to give up. He still thought he had some good fights left in him, even though his body was telling him otherwise.

So Gould got Braddock another fight, this one in San Francisco, at the Civic Auditorium, on September 21, 1932. Braddock was definitely cannon fodder for this bout, because he was facing the extremely promising light-heavyweight John Henry Lewis, who at the time was undefeated in 12 professional bouts, and who would eventually become the first African-American to hold the light-heavyweight title, an honour that he proudly held for more than four years.

Although the boxing world hadn't fully welcomed the black boxer at the time, Lewis came from a long lineage of boxers. His great-great uncle was Tom Molineaux, one of the first prominent bare-knuckle heavyweights, who had traveled to Great Britain to challenge for the boxing championship.

Lewis was born in California, but he'd moved to Arizona after his father was hired by the University of Arizona to be the trainer for the school's athletic teams. Lewis's father was also an astute boxing man, and he opened a gym in Phoenix.

At an early age, Lewis and his older brother Christy usually worked in their father's gym, fighting what was called "midget boxing" exhibitions. He then was taken on boxing-exhibition tours throughout the Southwest, and finally John Henry Lewis became a professional fighter, as a welterweight, at the tender age of 14.

At the age of 17, Lewis won the Arizona state middleweight championship. At 18, Lewis was already headlining this San Francisco card against a 26-year-old boxer who had once fought for the light-heavyweight title but had fallen on extremely tough times, a novice named Jim Braddock.

Braddock gave the teenager a game battle, but he was eventually outclassed and outpunched. Lewis had a solid 10-round decision that put him among the rising stars of the sport. Braddock had another payday of a little over $750, but he also had another loss, falling to 39-17. His hands were aching and his body was ravaged, but Gould found another payday for his fighter—and it came just nine days after the loss to Lewis. At this point, Gould and Braddock couldn't pick and choose. They had to take whatever was available.

Apparently, what was available was on the West Coast, because Braddock remained in California for the rest of

September and through November. Gould secured Braddock four fights in California. They weren't great paydays, about $750 per fight, but it was enough to survive on, and he could send some money home to Mae and the kids.

On September 30, Braddock was paired with a California heavyweight named Dynamite Jackson, a brawler who had just lost in his bid for the California heavyweight championship when his fight with a journeyman named Tom Patrick ended in the eighth round, at which point Jackson's cuts were too severe to continue. Patrick won the California crown, despite owning only a 12-11-3 record.

Jackson's career began with promise, but it was sidetracked when he developed a reputation as a bleeder.

Now, Jackson was getting a chance to revive his career a little if he could beat a recognizable fighter who'd once had a big name. The 10-round fight was scheduled as the lone event at the San Diego Coliseum.

Although Braddock was definitely considered a pushover for Jackson and entered the ring having lost six of his last seven bouts, he didn't show any signs of being an underdog. Braddock ignored the pain in his hand and pummeled Jackson with a series of rights over the final four rounds to earn a 10-round decision.

Once again, the win against a promising fighter gave the Braddock corner some hope. Maybe there would be better days ahead, financially, athletically. Rather than send him another step toward boxing oblivion, the win guaranteed him another gym, another payday, another shot, even if it was only to be beaten on by a contender.

On October 21, 1932, Gould sent Braddock into the ring against the reigning California heavyweight champion, Tom Patrick, who had defeated Jackson to earn the crown a few months earlier. The fight was to take place at Legion Stadium in Hollywood, with the idea that some of the major motion-picture moguls would be interested in attending a bout between the state's heavyweight champ and someone who was once a major name in the business.

The Braddock-Patrick fight was the lone event that night, a 10-round bout pitting boxers believed to be of equal talent. But Patrick hurt Braddock early in the fight, opening a cut over his right eye. The cut apparently wasn't severe enough to stop the fight, and Patrick earned a 10-round decision, dropping Braddock's record to 40-18.

After that loss, the 17th in 30 decisions, Braddock was forced to weigh some heavy options. He could go home to New Jersey and head back to the docks forever or try to continue the pursuit of a vanishing dream.

Gould tried to persuade his longtime friend to stick it out. After all, he already had a guaranteed purse for a final California fight, the headlining bout against Lou Scozza at the San Francisco Civic Auditorium, the same place where he'd been defeated by John Henry Lewis.

The Braddock-Scozza fight was going to be the main event on a six-bout fight card on November 9, 1932. Scozza was a Buffalo-based light-heavyweight who had once fought fellow Buffalonian Jimmy Slattery for the light-heavyweight crown, only to claim he was robbed of the 15-round decision.

In that Scozza-Slattery battle, held in Buffalo, legendary referee Arthur Donovan called the fight a draw, but two local judges ruled in favour of Slattery, even though Slattery had been knocked down in the 13th round and was apparently only saved by the bell.

The careers of Braddock and Scozza were almost parallel. They had both rolled through their early careers with a series of knockouts, then struggled in the years prior to their meeting. They had faced many of the same opponents, like Max Rosenbloom, who battled an amazing six times with Scozza, winning four times.

The most famous Scozza-Rosenbloom contest had occurred just four months prior to the Scozza-Braddock fight, on July 14, 1932. The bout was for the light-heavyweight title and was held at Bison Stadium in Buffalo.

Rosenbloom was his typical self. According to the *New York Times* report, "Slapsie Maxie" scored a ton of points in the early portion of the fight, "cuffing and slapping," as the report read. Encouraged by his hometown fans, Scozza tried valiantly to reverse the action and unleashed a full-fledged body-punch attack on the crafty Rosenbloom.

However, Rosenbloom knocked Scozza down with a jab in the seventh round, the lone knockdown of the fight. Scozza had the crowd of more than 10,000 enthused with a flurry of late-round punches, and they clamoured for a knockout that never came. Rosenbloom survived with a 15-round decision.

Two months later, Scozza had faced Rosenbloom again, this time in the Baseball Stadium in Montreal. Rosenbloom took a 10-round decision. A month later, Scozza went into the ring against the teenaged sensation John Henry Lewis and lost via unanimous decision. It was Scozza's eighth loss in 11 fights.

So when Scozza and Braddock finally met in November in San Francisco, it was a meeting of two fighters with similar résumés who were headed in the same direction—down.

Early in the fight, Scozza reopened the cut over Braddock's eye that he'd received in the fight against Patrick a month earlier. The blood flowed over Braddock's face, and there wasn't much that his cornermen could do to stop the bleeding.

Scozza, who wasn't much of a boxer, took advantage of the eye injury to batter Braddock. Finally, in the sixth round, referee Bennie Wagner stepped in and stopped the bout, awarding a technical-knockout victory to Scozza.

It stopped a five-fight losing streak for the boy from Buffalo.

Braddock headed home to New Jersey a thoroughly beaten boxer and a beaten man. It was not known how he could recover from this latest setback. In a career filled with rebounds and reinvention, any comeback this time would be beyond miraculous, almost of fairytale proportions.

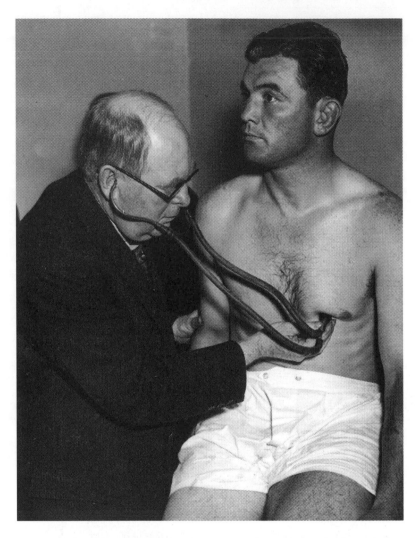

*Braddock sits in his shorts as Dr. William Walker listens to his heart during a medical checkup. (Photo by FPG/Getty Images)*

The United States of America had never been in more of a financial mess than it was as 1933 began. This was the worst of the Depression, and about 12,830,000 people, roughly 25 percent of the nation's total work force, were unemployed. More than 40 percent of the population was considered impoverished.

Even those who were fortunate enough to keep their jobs through the trying times watched their annual incomes fall at an average at a rate of 45 percent between 1929 and the beginning of 1933. Farm prices fell so drastically that many farmers lost their homes and land. Urban dwellers couldn't make their mortgage payments and lost their homes as well. Millions went hungry. Lines for free meals from soup kitchens went on for blocks, and many waited hours on end simply to get a slice of bread and a bowl of hot soup. It got so bad that families were forced to split up while the breadwinners tried desperately to find work any way they could.

"Hoovervilles," dubbed in jest against outgoing President Herbert Hoover, popped up all over the country in urban areas: impromptu shantytowns constructed of packing crates, discarded lumber, abandoned cars and other scraps.

Gangs of teenagers, who'd basically been discarded by families who couldn't afford to support them any longer, rode illegally on railroad cars like hoboes, hoping to find a job somewhere.

The millions of unemployed Americans were constantly on the move in search of their next dollar, but in reality, there really wasn't anywhere to go. Residents of Oklahoma, dubbed "Okies," endured drought and dust storms. Many thought it smart to pack up their families and head for California, where they believed jobs were plentiful, only to find nothing there for them.

The nation was virtually crippled. Factories closed. Steel mills and coal mines, staples of American industry at the turn of the century, were shut down and abandoned. Fortunes were lost.

Those who were unable to help themselves looked to the state and federal government for "relief," as welfare was called back then.

Disgusted, the American people elected Franklin Delano Roosevelt as the new President of the United States in 1932.

Within a few days of his landslide election, Roosevelt revealed a plan to get the nation out of the Great Depression. It was called the New Deal.

At the same time, in the months before FDR took the oath of office in March, 1933, Jim Braddock was also looking for a new deal—any deal.

The Depression had had its impact on the sport of boxing as well. The number of fight cards being produced around the country was dwindling. The chances for boxers to find work were decreasing and the purses were smaller.

Braddock's finances paralleled those of the nation. The family was dirt-poor. Working on the docks was sporadic. He could no longer afford to pay for his locker and training privileges at Joe Jeanette's gym, so he resorted to a dressing room above a West New York tavern to work out and remain in fighting shape. Joe Gould worked hard to get Braddock some guaranteed purses, but promoters were again shying away from Braddock.

Although he was relatively young at 27, the harbingers of one tough loss after another were beginning to show on Braddock. Still, he was not ready to face the inevitable, that his once-promising boxing career was coming to an end.

"I know I can still fight," Braddock told *Hudson Dispatch* sports editor Lud Shahbazian, who years later would write Braddock's authorized biography, *Relief to Royalty*. "I'm not ready to give up yet. I still have some good fights in me. I just have to somehow find them. But I know I can still fight. I know some people are beginning to call me a bum, but I don't think I am. I'm not done. I can't quit. I have a wife and family to take care of. They're the most important things in the world to me."

Especially since Mae was pregnant with the couple's third child.

Gould was able to get Braddock a fight on January 13, 1933, against Michigan-based light-heavyweight Martin Levandowski at the Chicago Stadium as part of the undercard that featured the featherweight-championship bout between Freddie Miller and Tommy Paul, won by Miller.

Levandowski was basically a light-heavyweight who wanted to explore the world of the heavyweights, so he took a step up to face Braddock, although Braddock had only a five-pound weight advantage (180 to 175). Levandowski came into the fight with a solid 23-4-2 record, and looked to be a formidable foe for Braddock.

But the inspired Braddock fought his best fight since his solid outing against Dynamite Jackson in San Diego the previous September. Braddock was in firm control from the outset and outscored Levandowski to earn the 10-round decision.

Gould was thinking again. Could this be yet another comeback? Could Braddock be back on the road toward respectability? It sure looked like it after the victory over Levandowski.

"Jimmy looked strong, real strong," Gould said to reporters after the bout. "No one could ever question Jimmy's heart. He's got the heart of a lion or a tiger. He just keeps coming."

One week after his fighter defeated Levandowski, Gould was able to convince Madison Square Garden promoters that Braddock could once again headline a big card. So the Garden promoters put Braddock atop a huge seven-bout card that featured top light-heavyweights Bob Olin and Abe Feldman.

Braddock was being paired with a bruising heavyweight from Hamburg, Germany named Hans Birkie, who came into the fight with a less-than-impressive 22-16-3 record against no real opponents of note. But Birkie did weigh 200 pounds, some 19 more than Braddock.

Birkie proved to be more than Braddock could handle. The powerful German kept Braddock at bay for most of the fight and hit him with a flurry of punches throughout the middle rounds. Braddock tried valiantly to recover in time to win the fight, but it was to no avail. Birkie, who ended his career with a sub-.500 record (36-40-7), outscored Braddock in a 10-round decision.

Braddock's career mark now stood at the very mediocre 41-20. Fighting for a championship was the furthest thing from his mind. Survival was more like it.

Gould was able to get Braddock more work, but he was back to the role of stepping-stone. Al Ettore was a promising heavyweight from Philadelphia, and promoters in the City of

Brotherly Love were looking for a warm body that Ettore could step over on his way up the heavyweight ladder.

That warm body was Jim Braddock. He was guaranteed $550 to take on the 5-0 Ettore in Philadelphia on March 1, 1933. In the fourth round of the fight, Braddock hit Ettore with a low blow, dropping Ettore to his knees. After Ettore received treatment, he decided he could not continue and Braddock was disqualified, giving Ettore the victory and dropping Braddock's record to 41-21.

Braddock was doing a tour of duty as an opponent to hometown heroes. He was given a date against St. Louis heavyweight Al Stillman on March 21, 1933, and faced Stillman in front of his local following at the St. Louis Arena. Stillman entered the fight with a 25-6-3 record and a three-bout winning streak. There were also approximately 4,000 avid St. Louis fight fans cheering wildly for the local boy.

But Braddock rallied late in the fight, putting Stillman to the canvas once in the ninth round and twice more in the 10th. Stillman tried to get back to his feet after the third knockdown, much to the delight of the audience, but referee Walter Heisner stopped the fight, giving Braddock a much-needed technical knockout victory.

Braddock returned home to West New York a victorious boxer. He greeted Mae with his $600 winnings. A day later, Braddock went straight to the docks to see if there was any work for him that day. There was none.

# 12

**B**y the inauguration of Franklin Delano Roosevelt as the new president of the United States in March 1933, the banking system in the country had been virtually eliminated.

Over the four years since the stock market crash of 1929, America's depositors had seen a total of $140 billion simply vanish because the banks that they did business with had failed. The credit system was shot. No one could get anything without cash in hand. Businesses could not get credit for inventory. Checks could not be used: some might be good, but others were totally worthless and there was no way to know the difference.

During the 1920s, an average of 70 U.S. banks failed each year. In the first 10 months of 1930 alone, 744 banks failed—10 times as many. By 1933, 9,000 banks had shut their doors. Many that remained open placed restrictions on how much money the depositors could withdraw. It caused a mass frenzy.

On Sunday, March 12, 1933, the third day after he took the oath of office, FDR declared a national "bank holiday," closing all banks in the country for three days. In the United Kingdom, a bank holiday was time for fun and frolic. In the U.S., it was a period of distress.

FDR took to the radio waves on that date to deliver what would become a regular feature in his incredible tenure as president, the national messages that he called his "fireside chats." It was FDR's way of calming the nation, of expressing his warmth and care by entering the nation's living rooms en route to becoming one of the nation's finest presidents ever. In that first address, he said:

*Your government does not intend that the history of the past few years shall be repeated. We do not want and will not have another epidemic of bank failures. It is necessary that the reopening of banks be extended over a period in order to permit the banks to make applications for the necessary loans, to obtain currency needed to meet their requirements, and to enable the government to make commonsense checkups. It is possible that when the banks resume, a very few people who have not recovered from their fear may again begin withdrawals. People will again be glad to have their money where it will be safely taken care of and where they can use it conveniently at any time. I can assure you, my friends, that it is safer to keep your money in a reopened bank than it is to keep it under the mattress. We had a bad banking situation. Some of our bankers had shown themselves either incompetent or dishonest in their handling of the people's funds. They had used the money entrusted to them in speculations and unwise loans. This was, of course, not true in the vast majority of our banks, but it was true in enough of them to shock the people of the United States for a time into a sense of insecurity and to put them into a frame of mind where they did not differentiate, but seemed to assume that the acts of a comparative few had tainted them all. And so it became the government's job to straighten out this situation and to do it as quickly as possible. And that job is being performed.*

*I do not promise you that every bank will be reopened or that individual losses will not be suffered, but there will be no losses that possibly could be avoided; and there would have been more and greater losses had we continued to drift. I can even promise you salvation for some at least of the sorely pressed banks. We shall be engaged not merely in reopening sound banks but in the creation of more sound banks through reorganization.*

*You people must have faith; you must not be stampeded by rumours or guesses. Let us unite in banishing fear. We have provided the machinery to restore our financial system; and it is up to you to support and make it work.*

*It is your problem, my friends, your problem no less than it is mine. Together we cannot fail. The only thing we have to fear is fear itself.*

Roosevelt didn't have the constitutional right to close the nation's banks, nor did he seek approval from the Senate or Congress. He just did it.

But luckless Americans put their collective faith in their newly elected and authorized leader. FDR's "bank holiday" and "fireside chat" kept the nation's chin up and got Americans moving. He kept the banking industry alive without having to nationalize it. He grabbed the support of the entire depressed nation with his calming words. With his New Deal, Roosevelt was going to ensure that the United States of America would survive as a capitalistic country and not move toward Communism, which was a deep fear at the time.

After the bank holiday and Roosevelt's speech, some banks reopened cautiously with strict limits on withdrawals. Thanks to FDR's plea, the American public didn't panic and ask to withdraw everything. Eventually, confidence returned to the system and banks were able to perform their economic function again.

To prevent similar disasters from ever happening again, the Federal Government established the Federal Deposit Insurance Corporation (FDIC), which eliminated the need for "bank runs"— crowds running to the bank before all the money ran out.

Backed by the FDIC, a bank could fail and go out of business, but then the government would reimburse depositors. The new plan also prevented banks from investing depositors' money in the stock market.

If FDR's New Deal and revised banking-system ideas had been in place five years earlier, Jim Braddock wouldn't have been in the deep financial predicament that he faced. During his heyday, he thought he was doing the right thing by investing much of his considerable earnings in what was believed to be a sure-fire stock market and putting the rest of his money in a savings account for Mae and his children. He was the antithesis of the typical Irish boxer of the 1920s and 30s, who often threw their money away on wine, women and song—and perhaps some whiskey as well. In fact, he once told a reporter that his greatest joy came when he was at home with Mae and the kids.

"I have the prettiest woman in the world who loves me," Braddock said. "And I have three great kids who I adore. What else could a man want?"

However, in the days after the bank holiday and FDR's famous speech, Braddock did have a want. It was called a lucky break.

That break might have come in the form of his stunning and impressive knockout of Al Stillman in Stillman's backyard of St. Louis. Braddock was going to get yet another chance to headline a card.

On April 5, 1933, Braddock was atop the marquee of a five-bout card at the St. Louis Arena, once again locking horns with Martin Levandowski, who he had defeated in a 10-round decision four months prior in Chicago.

It might have been too soon to give Levandowski a rematch: the Michigan-based light-heavyweight had not entered the ring since losing to Braddock on January 13. But Gould seized on the opportunity to make Braddock a headliner and to earn a decent purse, almost $900. It didn't seem like such a big risk, considering the earlier fight.

In the opening minutes of the fight, Braddock seemed to be in control and fired a straight right to Levandowski's chin. It missed the boxer's face, and hit him squarely in the shoulder. The awkward punch made Braddock wince in pain, he knew right away that something was seriously wrong.

"It's broken, Joe," Braddock said to Gould. "I know it. It always hurts, but it hasn't hurt like this in a while."

Gould was tempted to cut off Braddock's glove and throw in the towel to end the fight right there, but Braddock wouldn't allow it.

"Let me keep going," Braddock was overheard telling Gould. "I want to keep going, Joe. I can still beat this guy."

Relegated to using only his much weaker left hand, Braddock was rendered almost useless. He thought about using his mangled right hand, but the pain would have been too much to bear. So he gamely fought on with one hand and managed to score his share of points, but not enough. Braddock actually won on one judge's card, but Levandowski won the 10-round fight on a split decision.

Braddock's fears were correct. He had broken his right hand again with that awkward punch to Levandowski's shoulder. He went back home and had the hand examined by doctors. He didn't have enough money to have a specialist look at it. Actually, Braddock didn't want to go to any doctors, because he knew what they would recommend—either a six-month layoff or retirement. And he didn't want to hear any of that.

Braddock begged Gould to get him another fight right away. Gould was reluctant to do so, but Braddock persisted. They agreed that they needed the money. Gould said that he had a secret remedy that would heal Braddock's hand quicker: he would soak it in a liniment and mineral oil and then tightly wrap it with cloth. He'd heard, when he was learning about the fight game, even before he joined the Navy, that it worked for old boxers. Braddock felt it was worth a shot. Anything was.

*James J. Braddock (left) and Max Schmeling, conqueror of Joe Louis, sitting down at table together in New York City. Braddock is pointing to the right that Max used in pounding Louis into submission. (Photo © Corbis. All rights reserved.)*

# 13

After his loss to Martin Levandowski, Jim Braddock's career record stood at 42-22, which definitely ranked him in the mediocre class. He wasn't yet at the club-fighter stage, because he was still asked to headline cards like the one in St. Louis. But the injuries were mounting, especially the one to his badly broken right hand. The chances to earn the big-time paydays were seemingly gone. With work on the docks becoming rarer, Braddock began to wonder where the next dollar would come from.

"I wasn't fighting that much and I was working on the docks," Braddock said in *In This Corner*. "I had three kids and a wife I had to support. The family was growing up and I thought I had enough money to support them, you know, the food on the table and having a home. But things were a little rough, especially if the kids wanted anything. I guess with everyone at the time, things were tough. You'd find spots where you needed a little cash that you just didn't have."

Against his better judgment, because he knew his fighter was seriously hurt, Gould still managed to get Braddock another fight, just six weeks after breaking his hand in the loss to Levandowski. Of course, Gould knew that the hand hadn't properly healed, but if Braddock said he wanted to fight and there was a paycheck to be had, then Gould was going to give in to his fighter's wishes.

Again, Braddock would play the role of ring-filler for the hometown hero, and once again he was going to give a rematch to someone he'd already defeated: Al Stillman.

The rematch route didn't work against Levandowski, so why did Gould think it could be successful against Stillman, who still had a solid reputation as a contender and who'd given Braddock a good fight until the three late knockdowns, and who had just battled the active Max Rosenbloom to a hard-earned draw in April? The bout didn't make a lot of sense from the Braddock corner, except that it was another payday.

In the first round of the headline bout at the St. Louis Arena, Braddock found some magic in that injured right hand, knocking Stillman to the canvas and almost securing the 10-count that would have given him a knockout reminiscent of his early days, when nearly every one of his bouts ended in a first- or second-round punch-out.

But Stillman got up from the knockdown and recovered well. Meanwhile, the punch caused Braddock to wince and grasp his hand, looking disgusted.

Braddock knew that he'd hurt the hand badly again. When he'd delivered what looked like a knockout punch, he thought he might be able to walk out of the arena with a victory.

Once Stillman got up, Braddock knew it meant trouble. As in the second fight against Levandowski, he was not going to be able to use the right hand for the rest of the bout. He tried to gamely lead with his right and follow through with his left, but it wasn't the right time for an old dog to learn new tricks. He was headed for yet another defeat.

For some reason, only two judges voted in the fight. The referee's card was never counted. Levandowski scored more points on both judges' cards and earned the unanimous decision. For the first time in his career, Braddock was beginning to feel like a beaten man. At 42-23, he did not have the record of any boxer of note.

After Braddock's two one-handed losses, Gould asked him if he was ready to walk away.

The answer was simple.

"No way, Joe," Braddock said. "No way."

Despite the injuries, despite the losses, Braddock wanted to trudge on. Mae Braddock backed her man 100 per cent, and even though he knew better, Gould also continued to support his friend.

"I've always believed in you, Jimmy," Gould said. "I'm not going to quit now. If you want to keep fighting, I'm with you, every step of the way."

The two continued to train in the little room over the West New York bar. Gould continued to look for fights. They were giving persistence a new meaning.

On the days that Braddock wasn't training, he tried to get work at the docks. Every day presented a new challenge. Some days, as many as 20 workers were needed. Some days, as few as five were called. Still, you had to be there every day to see if you would be selected.

At the docks, Braddock wasn't known as a former light-heavyweight boxing contender. There, he was just like everyone else, a desperate man looking to earn a simple day's pay.

The foremen who picked the dockworkers preferred the fitter, younger men, so Braddock had a good shot of being selected, because he was relatively healthy. He didn't ask for favours and never told anyone at the docks who he was, for fear that the other workers would resent him, thinking he was getting preferential treatment. Down at the docks, he was just a strapping young man willing to work.

A month after losing to Stillman, Braddock signed on for a bout, one that he was finally going to fight in his own backyard. Gould got Braddock a fight on June 21, 1933 against Les Kennedy at Boyle's Thirty Acres in Jersey City, the site of the Jack Dempsey-Georges Carpentier title fight in 1921.

Kennedy, a native of Long Beach, California, had had the misfortune of meeting the Italian behemoth Primo Carnera six months earlier and becoming a third-round knockout victim. (One week after the Braddock-Kennedy fight, the 6-5, 260-pound Carnera would knock out Jack Sharkey in the sixth round at the Madison Square Garden Bowl in Long Island City, N.Y. to capture the heavyweight championship of the world.) In his last fight prior to facing Braddock, the 36-16-2 Kennedy had a controversial fight with Jersey City heavyweight Stanley Poreda, who was knocked down in the ninth round and remained down so long that Kennedy's handlers entered the ring, only to realize that the referee had not completed the count. Poreda was able to continue, but Kennedy won via technical knockout a round later.

Kennedy also owned a victory in 1930 against an up-and-coming heavyweight named Max Baer, who Kennedy reportedly handled easily. At the time, it was only the second loss suffered by Baer, who would defeat Carnera in 1934 to capture the world heavyweight title.

Braddock and Kennedy had had several common opponents between them: Kennedy owned a win over Baxter Calmes, who'd defeated Braddock a year earlier. But Kennedy had also been beaten twice by Dynamite Jackson, who Braddock had beaten in 1932. Both boxers had losses at the hands of Leo Lomski and Charley Retzlaff.

So there really wasn't any way to guess the outcome of the bout beforehand based on past performances and common opponents. It seemed to be a fairly even bout, and one that would certainly draw a few people, considering that Braddock was finally the hometown hero.

However, the gate was something of a disappointment; Braddock gained less than $1,000.

Braddock was the aggressor from the outset, even though he was still not able to fully use his right hand. This was an occasion on which Braddock was more of a boxer than a brawler. His strategy was to use the left jab over and over, to the point where one local sportswriter dubbed him "Jabbin' Jim."

The approach seemed to work. Braddock managed to pile up points throughout the middle rounds, much to the delight of the faithful following. He never had a chance to put Kennedy away, but he scored enough points to secure a well-earned 10-round decision, improving his record to 43-23.

The victory was enough to get Braddock another headlining fight, again in his hometown, against a quintessential journeyman heavyweight from Brooklyn named Chester Matan, who was in even worse decline as a boxer than Braddock.

Matan was signed to face Braddock on July 21, 1933, even though Matan had lost nine straight bouts against some less-than-stellar opponents and had dropped 11 of his last 12. This time Matan was facing the hometown hero in the same fashion that Braddock did in the bouts against Al Ettore in Philly and Al Stillman in St. Louis.

Ironically, Matan's first professional fight in 1930 had been against a New Jersey-based heavyweight named Charlie Wepner, whom Matan defeated.

Charlie Wepner was the father of Chuck Wepner, who gained fame as "The Bayonne Bleeder," and who fought Muhammad Ali for the heavyweight title in 1975 and was allegedly the inspiration Sylvester Stallone used when he wrote the screenplay for the Academy Award-winning movie *Rocky*.

Matan proved to be no match for Braddock, who pounded him with a series of punches, using both hands, and rolled to an easy 10-round decision. Braddock now had two wins in a row.

No other boxer in the sport's history had been through such highs and lows before. But it was all just a precursor of what was to follow.

*Tommy Farr (left), British Heavyweight Champion and James J Braddock. (Photo by Keystone/Getty Images)*

# 14

After Jim Braddock thrilled his hometown fans with the win over Matan, he found that there wasn't much interest for his services as a boxer.

It was the height of the outdoor boxing season, with all the big outdoor venues getting ready to put on shows. But there were no calls from the promoters who used to reach out for Braddock on a regular basis.

At the same time, Braddock was now lucky if he got one day a week as a dockworker. Sometimes, he went religiously to the docks every single day, only to be turned away.

Sometimes, the foreman was there, ready to pick workers, but the work orders never arrived. So prospective workers like Braddock would stand there for hours, awaiting the word that never came. Braddock would give up after three or four hours and return home to Mae and the kids.

Braddock was definitely a family man. He loved to play with his children at every chance, shadow-boxing with Jay, playing hide-and-seek with Rose Marie. He adored Mae and relished every minute they were together.

Braddock also appreciated his wife's unwavering support. No matter what he chose to do, she was going to be by his side. She didn't push or prod him about possibly walking away from boxing. She could see the pain and anguish that he was in whenever he came home, the body aches, the bruised and battered midsection, the mangled hand. Of course, Mae Braddock wanted her husband to be healthy and happy. That was first and foremost. But she also knew that Jim actually loved boxing. He loved being with Joe Gould, loved being with the other people he met along the way. He appreciated the relationships he developed over the years with such prominent boxing figures as Jack Dempsey and Mickey Walker, people whom Braddock had admired when he was younger.

So if Jim Braddock truly believed he could still box, that was fine in the eyes of Mae Braddock. He wasn't going to quit. He had just turned 27 years old. He felt he had something left.

There were no fights in August. It was good, Braddock believed, because he was giving the hand some time to heal.

Gould's home remedy wasn't helping much. One doctor told Braddock that the only way to have the hand heal properly was through surgery. But Braddock didn't have health insurance and didn't have the money to pay for a proper office visit, never mind surgery.

Braddock just gritted his teeth and moved on, trying to train as much as possible to keep in shape, while trying to work as much as possible as well. The training was easy. The work on the docks was not.

After Braddock had gone a few weeks without getting picked to work, someone suggested that he should apply for relief from the New Jersey Division of Welfare.

Braddock, ever the stubborn and proud Irishman, would hear nothing of the idea. He firmly believed that there were others who needed the help from the government more than he did.

But the Braddock family situation wasn't getting any better. The rent was not being paid. Nor were the utility bills.

Pride or no pride, Braddock had to do something. Mae Braddock told her husband that it was fine for the time being to accept the relief funds. She insisted that it was only temporary. Finally, Braddock agreed to make an appointment with the Welfare Department—until Gould told Braddock of another fight he had lined up.

It was a benefit night for the Mount Vernon Police Department's Home Relief Fund, with heavyweight champ Primo Carnera making an appearance as a guest referee and Braddock headlining the six-bout card at Memorial Field Stadium in Mount Vernon, New York on September 25, 1933.

Braddock's opponent that night was Abe Feldman, a Jewish fighter born in Salt Lake City and raised in New York. Feldman was an up-and-comer with an impressive 18-1 record and had just defeated Hans Birkie two weeks earlier. Birkie was the brawny heavyweight who'd soundly defeated Braddock earlier that year.

This would definitely not be a pushover fight for Braddock.

In the early rounds against Feldman, Braddock connected with his right hand, but once again he could tell that something was severely wrong. He had broken his fragile right hand one more time.

Doctors had warned Braddock that the hand would not heal properly without corrective surgery. Now, the hand was so bad that he simply could not continue. The pain was excruciating. Braddock looked to Gould and asked him to call the referee over and examine the hand. The referee realized that Braddock could not continue, and after the sixth round was completed, the ref stopped the bout and called it a non-contest.

When the New York State Athletic Commission required that Braddock provide medical evidence that his hand was indeed broken in order to receive his $650 for participating in the fight, Braddock couldn't. He didn't have the money to see a doctor, so he never received his fee.

With his hand now hurt worse than ever before and with its only hope for recovery coming in the form of reconstructive surgery, Braddock was faced with the biggest decision of his professional boxing career.

After talking it over with Mae and with Joe Gould, Braddock decided the obvious. He was through with boxing. He was going to retire. There was really no sense to continue, to prolong the agony. He had given it his all. He had won more bouts than he lost. He had had a shot at a title. It had been a good career, he thought.

Braddock figured he could try to make the most of it at the docks. And in the meantime, yes, he would take the advice of others and accept assistance. The dreaded "relief" was going to become a part of the Braddock lifestyle. He would accept welfare.

Braddock went to the New Jersey Department of Welfare office in Jersey City, where his case was reviewed. With a wife and three children, Braddock was eligible to receive $24 a month. That was it. He was going to have to support his entire family on a measly 24 bucks.

Around the same time, there were reports that the famed Irish gangster, Owen "Owney" Madden, was prepared to buy Braddock's contract and "own" his personal services for a regular fee. Madden was known for being the owner and proprietor of the famed Cotton Club in Harlem, where he employed great musical legends like Duke Ellington and Lena Horne.

Madden, who came to prominence as a master brewer

and bootlegger during the Prohibition era in New York, was also reportedly the lover of actress Mae West and the silent producer of her Broadway shows. He also reportedly gave boyhood friend George Raft his big break in Hollywood.

Madden tended to exaggerate a bit, and he liked to brag to newspaper reporters. He claimed that he'd influenced a lot of conventioneers to get FDR nominated at the Democratic National Convention in Chicago in 1932.

So when Madden boasted to reporters in 1933 that he owned both Braddock and heavyweight champ Primo Carnera, everyone in the newspaper industry winced in disbelief.

When Braddock received word of Madden's claim, he just shrugged his shoulders. "If he owns me, then I hope he's paying me," Braddock reportedly said to a family friend.

Everyone who knew Jim Braddock knew one thing: He would never do anything dishonest, and he certainly wasn't going to sell his soul to one of the kingpins of organized crime.

It didn't matter that both Madden and Braddock were Irish and that Madden had more money than he could count. In Braddock's eyes, Madden's money was blood money. He'd rather be working on the docks for next to nothing and collecting welfare than dealing with someone as seedy as Owney Madden.

Braddock was going to go back to the docks and earn an honest wage—if there was a wage to be had there.

# 15

**W**hen Jim Braddock couldn't collect his purse for the fight against Abe Feldman and headed back to the docks for sporadic work as a stevedore in late September of 1933, he was convinced that boxing was behind him. He had stopped training and was concentrating on finding regular work as a longshoreman. But he had another problem: he wasn't able to use his right hand at all.

One day, Braddock was asked to bale hay from a freighter. But his mangled right hand was useless, so he took the baling hook with his left hand and managed to pick up the 150-pound bales with relative ease.

The foremen on the job were amazed at Braddock's brute strength working with just one hand. He was able to use his left arm with an uncanny, fluid motion, like there was nothing to it. Over and over, bend and throw, bend and throw. With every throw, his left arm got stronger and stronger. It was better than any weight training technique that Joe Gould could ever have taught his boxer.

After a few days of using the same motion, Braddock noticed a dramatic improvement in the strength of his left arm. He continued to use the technique any time he was selected to work.

Braddock also continued to collect the monthly $24 in welfare assistance. He needed every dime he could get. Sure, he was embarrassed by having to stand on the line and collect the pittance. One time, Braddock asked someone else to sign his name on the "relief roll," because his hand hurt so much—and also because he was mortified that someone he knew might notice him collecting welfare.

The gas was turned off in the Braddock home as winter approached. To keep the family safe and warm, the children were moved to a relative's house. Jim Braddock didn't want to lose his children, and he was very hopeful that the move was temporary. He believed his luck would change—some way, somehow.

After all, Braddock was the comeback kid. He'd made countless comebacks in the ring when everyone had counted him out for good. Why couldn't he make a comeback in life?

Braddock was a man of deep religious faith, a devout Irish Catholic, and he considered several priests close friends, including those in the rectory at St. Joseph of the Palisades in West New York. When times were at their toughest, Braddock would head to the residence and seek advice.

There were no tougher times than the fall and winter of 1933 into 1934. Braddock was virtually penniless. His children had been taken from him. He had no gas heat in the family flat.

The priests at St. Joseph all told Jim to keep his faith; that God would provide him the strength to carry on. Braddock heeded the advice. Nothing was going to deter Braddock's faith. Nothing.

Braddock began to borrow a few dollars here and there from friends, from anyone, to get by. Joe Gould gave him a few bucks that he didn't have to spare. The two had traveled the tumultuous boxing road together. That association wasn't about to end now, even if Braddock was away from the ring.

"If you want me to, Jimmy, I'll keep looking for fights for you," Gould said one day during the winter months of early 1934. "I'm not ready to give up on you."

Braddock thought about it. He knew that there was still money to be made in the ring. His right hand was healing, or so he thought. The pain wasn't as intense now, and his left arm was stronger than ever.

"If you can find something, Joe, then we'll do it," Braddock said. "Make sure it's a good one, if you get it."

Even though he wasn't working, Gould had to be around the boxing game. So he would go to Madison Square Garden on a regular basis, just to talk with the trainers, managers and promoters that he'd become friendly with over the years.

In early June, 1934, Gould overheard Madison Square Garden promoter Jimmy Johnston talking to someone about needing an opponent for the promising heavyweight John "Corn" Griffin, a massive, powerful puncher from Fort Benning, Georgia. The original opponent had backed out, and Johnston needed someone to fill out the card, which was going to be highlighted by the heavyweight-title fight between champion Primo Carnera and challenger Max Baer.

"Why not Jimmy Braddock?" Gould asked Johnston.

Johnston laughed.

"Braddock's done, finished," Johnston said. "I can't put him in the ring against Griffin. He'll get killed."

Gould implored and begged Johnston to give Braddock another shot.

"This will be the last chance," Gould said. "Give Jimmy one last chance."

Johnston really didn't have another choice. He was desperate. The card was scheduled for June 14 at the Madison Square Garden Bowl in Long Island City. It was a seven-bout card that featured familiar names like Dynamite Jackson, Al Ettore and Chester Matan, all former Braddock foes. Plus, there was a heavyweight title on the line, so that meant a huge crowd—40,000 spectators, maybe more. He needed someone he could throw to a wolf like Corn Griffin who would serve as a human punching bag. He needed a bum.

Johnston reluctantly gave in. He promised Gould a purse of $250.

Gould asked for a little more, but Johnston was adamant: Take the $250 or forget it. Gould took it. It was money. It was better than nothing. It was a chance to put some food on the table.

Gould went back to New Jersey and pulled Braddock away from the docks. He told him he had a fight for him— in two days.

Braddock hadn't stepped into the ring since he'd decided to walk away from the sport nine months earlier after the no-contest against Abe Feldman. Now he had all of two days to prepare to face Griffin, who had knocked the champ Carnera around pretty regularly when the two sparred. Griffin was known for his monstrous left hook, a punch that had pulverized a solid light-heavyweight named George Manley earlier that year. And Braddock had to be rusty, having been away from the ring for so long.

"He was a left hooker and I always had a lot of success with left hookers," Braddock told Peter Heller.

"I had a fast right hand and if you're coming in with a left hook and you meet a guy with a right hand, you can hit him in the right spot," Braddock said. "Joe told me that I had a shot to win."

Things didn't look good for Braddock early on against Griffin. He walked into one of Griffin's rights, and he went down. Gould figured that was it. His one shot at making yet another comeback was done within six minutes.

"He hit me with a right hand behind the ear," Braddock said. "He put me on the deck."

But Gould's fighter managed to get to his feet at the eighth count and seemed to find himself right away. In fact, Braddock scored several times with his right hand before the end of the second round and continued the barrage into the third.

In the third round, Braddock was powerful with the right hand, just like he figured he would be against a left hooker.

"I hit him right on the chin and that was it," Braddock said. "He was rated a pretty good fighter at that time."

Braddock had a third-round technical knockout. The referee stopped the fight at the 2:37 mark. Incredibly, the comeback kid had done it again, winning a fight that no one gave him a chance to win.

Later that day, Baer totally humiliated the huge Italian Carnera, knocking him down an incredible 11 times in 11 rounds to earn an 11th-round technical knockout and snatching his world heavyweight title.

While many people left the Madison Square Garden Bowl that day talking about the new heavyweight champion, the biggest surprise of the day had come at the hands of Jim Braddock. Boxing experts wondered whether

Braddock had one more legitimate comeback in him or if the impressive win over contender Griffin was just a flash in the pan.

The $250 payday, the worst since Braddock's extremely early days as a professional, provided some food and enabled Braddock to have the gas turned back on in his apartment. It was still a far cry from the $5 a day working at the docks or the $24 he would get monthly from welfare.

But the win over Griffin proved one thing. Braddock still had some fight in him. He wasn't a complete washout at age 28.

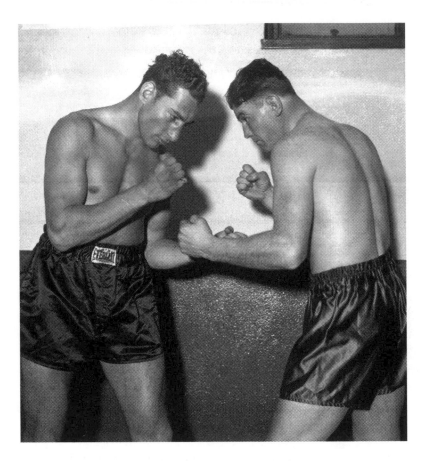

*Art Lasky, (left) and Jimmy Braddock, (right) square off for cameramen March 22, 1935 prior to their bout in Madison Square Garden. Lasky weighed in at 197 pounds and Braddock at 182 for the scheduled 15 rounder. (AP Photo / Walter Durkin)*

# 16

Jim Braddock's stunning and dominating victory over Corn Griffin propelled him back into the boxing mainstream. He had the motivation to get back into the ring and train more rigorously. He had the encouragement of his wife. With the miraculous recovery to his right hand and his newfound power and strength in his left, Braddock was indeed a new boxer. He was now even more complete, not having to rely on the powerful right to win. He had two lethal hands. For what had to be at least the 10th time in his career, Braddock had reinvented himself.

The Griffin victory was enough to allow Joe Gould to have an audience with promoters once again.

Gould arranged another fight for Braddock, and again, it appeared to be a losing proposition. Gould set up a bout with the top contender John Henry Lewis, who had knocked Braddock silly in a 10-round decision in San Francisco in September of 1932. Lewis was now at the top of *The Ring* magazine's rankings, as the top-ranked light-heavyweight on his way to the crown, but he wanted a chance to get the bigger paydays that the heavyweights demanded.

On paper, this was simply a fight that Braddock could not win. Beating Griffin was one thing. Corn Griffin was unrefined, a puncher. Lewis, who'd only lost once in 32 professional fights (he'd lost to Rosenbloom, only to come back and beat the affable Jewish fighter twice in a span of four months), had all the attributes of a great boxer. He had the speed of a welterweight and was as aggressive as a heavyweight. He was proficiently skilled at defense and packed a powerful punch. Plus, he was still only 20 years old.

Lewis was clearly on the rise, and Braddock was on the way down. It appeared as if Braddock was being used as cannon fodder for yet another contender. In fact, Lewis won the light-heavyweight title a year later, the first African-American to ever hold the crown, and he held the belt for four years. He eventually became a member of the International Boxing Hall of Fame, having won 107 fights in his career and having lost only eight.

But the bout with Lewis, scheduled for November 16, 1934 at Madison Square Garden, represented a better payday for Braddock and Gould. The manager secured $700 for Braddock for fighting Lewis, on the undercard of a four-bout night headlined by the Max Rosenbloom-Bob Olin bout for the light-heavyweight championship of the world, which Olin won by unanimous decision.

Being heavy underdogs didn't distract Braddock and Gould. They trained hard and long, and Braddock entered the ring, with the odds almost 5-to-1 against him, but claiming he was in the best shape of his life.

It showed. In the fifth round, Braddock unleashed a barrage of punches and nailed Lewis with a stunning right, sending him to the canvas. Everyone in attendance was thoroughly shocked. Lewis had never been knocked down before in his career. (He would only be knocked down once more—by Joe Louis, five years later.)

Dazed, Lewis got back on his feet and continued to fight, but Braddock had obviously hurt him and continued to dominate the last five rounds, winning the decision.

Braddock had performed the unthinkable, defeating two top-ranked contenders in a span of six months after being away from boxing completely for nearly a year.

Soon after the win over Lewis, legendary promoter Mike Jacobs announced that he was instituting a heavyweight elimination tournament, pitting all the top heavyweight contenders in bouts that would eventually lead to the heavyweight championship.

Gould begged Jacobs to include Braddock in the tournament. After Braddock's two previous performances, fights that were getting Braddock a little buzz and excitement among fans, Jacobs agreed.

But once again, Braddock was being thrown to the wolves. He was being paired against Art Lasky, the No. 1 contender for the heavyweight championship.

Born Arthur Lakofsky in Minneapolis (it was common for boxers' names to get changed at the whim of managers), Lasky was a fit heavyweight who'd gained his reputation fighting mostly in his native Minnesota and in California. He was known for a powerful right hand and a devastating knockout punch. Lasky had won nine straight fights via knockout in 1933 and 1934. The 24-year-old was a rising star.

Braddock and Gould didn't care. This was the big time. If Braddock mustered yet another miraculous victory, it would pave the way for a shot at the heavyweight crown. Or so it seemed.

"In reality, there was no real talk of a heavyweight championship fight for me, because they figured Lasky would lick me," Braddock told Peter Heller.

Lasky, who was managed by his father, Maurice, didn't want to fight Braddock, because he didn't think a win over Braddock would mean anything. Sure, it was part of the elimination tournament, and a win would continue Lasky's ascent toward a title bout, but Lasky figured that Braddock was a downtrodden boxer who he'd simply be expected to beat. Lasky had a bigger prize in his sights—a showdown with Max Baer for the heavyweight title.

Braddock faced Lasky as the headlining bout in a five-bout card at Madison Square Garden on March 22, 1935. Braddock had a major weight disadvantage, weighing 182 to Lasky's 197.

Lasky had a reputation of being a slow starter, and Braddock seized on that opportunity. He came after Lasky with a flurry of rights and lefts. Since he'd begun to use his left hand more frequently, Braddock had really become a totally different fighter. It was also amazing to see the new power in the left.

Braddock took control of the fight early on and never relinquished it.

"I hit him with everything," Braddock said. "I mean, wherever his kisser was, I hit him. I had a punch for everything. A left hook, a right cross. . . . It was one of my better nights."

Lasky couldn't recover from the battering he received from the rejuvenated Braddock. The outcome was just as shocking as the previous two Braddock bouts had been. Braddock soundly defeated the Minnesotan, who had entered the ring with an impressive 32-4-3 record, in a unanimous decision.

Braddock received $4,100 for defeating Lasky—more than he'd earned in the previous two years combined. There was no more need to stand on the welfare lines. In fact, Braddock went to the New Jersey Department of Welfare to repay the money that he'd been given over the prior 18 months.

"They had paid me, so I returned it," Braddock said to Heller. "I figured that they could give it to somebody else who needed it, because they were good enough to give it to me when I needed it. I was in a spot where I could finally pay it back."

Braddock was able to repay some of his other old debts, too. He didn't have to go back to the docks. His children moved back home. Things were finally looking up.

They were only going to get better.

Damon Runyon became fascinated with Braddock's amazing story, from the welfare lines and the brink of despair to heavyweight title contender. In an article written after the Lasky fight, Runyon called Braddock, "the Cinderella Man."

The moniker stuck. It was far better than the "Plain James" that John Kiernan of the *New York Times* used to describe Braddock. After all, every boxer had to have a nickname. Baer was the "Livermore Larupper." Jack Dempsey was the "Manassas Mauler." Primo Carnera was the "Ambling Alp."

Plain James, Jersey Jim—those names weren't going to work anymore, especially when a figure like Runyon dubs you with a new one. Braddock was forever to be known as "the Cinderella Man."

It was a nickname that fitted like a glove.

# 17

"I was the pauper," Jim Braddock told Peter Heller, "And then, I was the prince." In the span of just nine months, Jim Braddock went from being a broke dockworker on welfare to being a heavyweight-title contender. The string of three impressive victories over Corn Griffin, John Henry Lewis and Art Lasky had done exactly that.

Gould figured that if top promoters like Jacobs were pushing Lasky for a possible title fight against Baer, why didn't his fighter deserve a title shot now? Braddock certainly deserved the shot, Gould believed.

After the victory over Lasky, Braddock moved to No. 2 in the heavyweight-contender rankings. The No. 1

contender was the imposing German Max Schmeling, the former heavyweight champion who'd lost his title to Jack Sharkey in 1932. Jacobs initially wanted Schmeling to fight Braddock, with the winner to get a shot at Baer.

But Schmeling figured he deserved a shot at Baer without having to go through Braddock to get it, so he refused to fight Braddock. Schmeling would have to wait for his chance to get another crack at the heavyweight crown.

So Jacobs reluctantly agreed with Gould that Braddock should replace Lasky in the scheme of things.

The deal was set up. Braddock was signed to fight Baer for the heavyweight championship of the world, in a fight scheduled to be held at the Madison Square Garden Bowl on June 13, 1935. As the champion, Baer would receive 42 percent of the overall gate. Braddock would get 15 percent.

With the overall gate (including radio-broadcast rights) estimated anywhere between $350,000 and $400,000, Braddock was looking at a payday of approximately $50,000 to $60,000. There would be no more need for "relief." In addition to a slew of contenders, Jim Braddock had beaten the Great Depression as well.

Every boxing expert now figured that Braddock had absolutely no shot against Baer. This wasn't Griffin or Lewis or even Lasky. This was the vaunted heavyweight champ, the fearsome Max Baer.

On the day he signed for the fight, Braddock was listed as a 10-to-1 underdog. It was believed that no one could survive Baer's powerful right hand. After all, Baer had been credited as actually killing two men in the ring, and it was then believed that he, and not Primo Carnera, had inflicted the fatal blows to Ernie Schaaf. That would have meant that Baer actually killed three opponents while boxing.

The first death had come early in Baer's career, in Oakland, California on September 25, 1929. In just his ninth professional fight, Baer pummeled a non-descript club fighter named Frank Rudzenski in the third round, knocking him through the ropes with a vicious left hook. The referee didn't stop Baer, who continued to hit Rudzenski while he was hanging onto the ropes, finally knocking him clear out of the ring. The head injuries suffered by Rudzenski would prove to be fatal. He died three weeks later.

Exactly 11 months later, on August 25, 1930, a similar incident took place, this time in San Francisco against an up-and-coming heavyweight with a 33-3-2 record named Frankie Campbell.

According to a published report by United Press International about the fight, Baer slugged Campbell "unmercifully" after he was already clearly unconscious but able to somehow remain standing by wrapping his feet in the ropes.

After the referee Toby Irwin allowed Baer's savage beating to continue, the fight was eventually stopped. Doctors worked on Campbell inside the ring for about half an hour but failed to revive him. Campbell was transported to a local hospital, where other doctors worked on him for several hours. According to the doctor's report, Campbell died from a severe concussion that caused his brain to swell to three times its normal size.

The California State Athletic Commission soon suspended referee Irwin for his failure to stop the fight, as well as J. Hamilton Lorimer (Baer's manager), Carol E. Working and Tom Maloney (Campbell's managers), and the trainers and handlers for both boxers.

Finally, there was the fight with Schaaf. It was usually believed that Carnera's blows had killed Schaaf, because Schaaf died just four days after fighting the massive Italian on February 10, 1933 at Madison Square Garden.

But others firmly believed that the damage was done in the August 31, 1932 fight in Chicago between Baer and Schaaf. In the final seconds of the 10th and final round, Baer was savagely beating Schaaf when the bell rang, ending the fight and preventing Baer from earning a knockout win, although he did win handily on points. Schaaf was totally unconscious after the fight, flat on his face for three minutes, before his handlers got him to his feet.

Because there was no medical condition at the time, Schaaf was never officially examined for any head injuries after the Baer fight, and he fought three more times before entering the ring against Carnera.

Witnesses say that the punches thrown by Carnera to take down Schaaf were straight jabs, not of the knockout variety. But Schaaf crumpled to the canvas, and was taken to a New York hospital where emergency brain surgery was performed to remove a blood clot from his brain and to lessen the inflammation. It didn't work, and Schaaf died four days later.

Baer had earned a reputation as a surly, nasty beast, and he inspired fear in practically everyone in the boxing game, especially after the way he totally dismantled the huge Carnera the year before, but Braddock was not one bit afraid. He always thoroughly believed he could beat Baer. He might have been a dismal underdog in the eyes of oddsmakers and boxing experts—a mere pushover on Baer's road to immortality—but not in his own mind.

From the minute he put his name to the contract, securing the fight, Braddock had every intention of winning. In fact, Braddock was so confident that he spent his purse money, buying Mae and the kids a new luxurious house in nearby North Bergen, New Jersey, overlooking a spacious green park.

Braddock remembered going to Madison Square Garden on February 6, 1931, to see Baer fight Tommy Loughran, a bout that was refereed by Jack Dempsey.

Although it had been four years since that fight, Braddock recalled the way the smaller Loughran jabbed and peppered Baer into frustration. Baer looked to land his monstrous right throughout the fight, but the left-handed craftsman from Philly, who destroyed Braddock in similar fashion in the light-heavyweight championship fight in

1929, kept Baer at bay with scoring punches en route to an easy 10-round decision.

"I had seen Tommy Loughran lick Baer in the Garden," Braddock told Heller. "I had boxed Tommy and I knew what kind of a boxer he was and I said to myself that if I ever got a chance to fight Baer, then I would do the same thing. I'd lead with my left hand and move. That was my plan."

Braddock had also had a lot of confidence in his left hand ever since his impromptu workouts at the docks.

The press conference announcing the fight was surreal and probably set the tone for future press conferences because of all the flamboyance and chicanery performed by Baer, who had a good sense of humor and loved to put on a show for the reporters. In fact, Baer, whose son Buddy would later gain fame as Jethro on the popular US sitcom, *The Beverly Hillbillies*, always aspired to become an actor, even before he entered the ring.

Baer had earned a reputation as "The Clown Prince of Boxing" with his jovial antics in and out of the ring. He would ham it up for the audience, wave to people, smile, fool around. Famous boxing writer John Kiernan of the *New York Times* called Baer "the hilarious Harlequin of Hollywood." When the writers were nearby, poised with their notepads and pencils, and the camera bulbs were popping, Baer was quick with a joke or a prank that always drew a laugh.

Baer cracked lines about looking forward to his future fight against Joe Louis, totally ignoring Braddock.

When someone asked Baer about Braddock's chances in the fight, Baer replied, "Jimmy's a nice man. Everyone likes Jimmy. But let's face facts. Jimmy is Jimmy."

Braddock was a little more subdued. He remained confident, but he didn't want to brag. When reporters asked him about being down in the dumps, about being on welfare, about truly becoming "the Cinderella Man," Braddock said, "I believe we live in a great country. It's a country that is good enough to help a man in trouble, help him when he's down. I had a run of bad luck, but I have a lot to be grateful for. I have the prettiest wife in the world and three healthy, troublemaking kids. I guess I'm just grateful for the opportunity, because these days, not everyone gets a second chance."

Those words would begin to endear James Walter Braddock, or James J. Braddock as Joe Gould had renamed him, to the entire world.

*American boxer Max Baer and Italian boxer Primo Carnera during the bout for the Heavyweight Championship, Long Island City, New York, June 14, 1934. Baer won on a technical knockout after 11 rounds. (Photo by American Stock / Getty Images)*

# 18

I n May of 1935, both Max Baer and Jim Braddock went to New York's Catskill Mountains to train for their June 13 heavyweight-championship fight. Yes, Braddock was actually getting a regular training-camp facility. There was no need to use the tiny room over the bar in West New York. This was a big-time training camp with a slew of trainers and handlers.

Before Braddock went off to Loch Sheldrake, New York for the month-long preparation, his nephew approached him in the bar/training facility in West New York. The seven-year-old Joe Mallon, named after his uncle Joe Braddock, who had introduced Jim Braddock to boxing, pinned a religious medal to one of his uncle's boxing shoes.

"Good luck, Champ," little Joe Mallon said.

Braddock was diligent and determined in his preparation, working eight to 10 hours a day. One of the trainers called in to work with Braddock was a young fellow from New York named Ray Arcel, who learned how to be a good "cut man" from working with Gene Tunney's manager, Frank "Doc" Bagley.

It was the first time Arcel ever trained a heavyweight in his career, which would eventually cover 60 years of work with stars and champions like Ezzard Charles, Roberto Duran and Larry Holmes.

On the other hand, Baer was lackadaisical, having just returned from an exhibition tour to capitalize on being the champion and to promote the Braddock fight. His camp was a circus, filled with celebrities like actors Clark Gable, Errol Flynn and John Barrymore. There was no way Baer could take his opponent seriously. He spoke of Joe Louis and a possible $1 million purse. He trained very little, sometimes never entering the ring at all.

In the days prior to the fight, Baer told reporters, "I feared for Braddock's safety . . . I think I could actually kill him."

Mae Braddock read those words and cringed. She wasn't a big boxing fan and had often feared for her husband's safety. Now he was facing a man who had a reputation as a killer. Was he safe? Was she about to lose her man in the ring?

Jim Braddock called home and reassured Mae that everything would turn out fine.

"Honey, relax," he said. "I'm going to make history."

Five days before the fight, Braddock was interviewed by New York Times reporter Joseph C. Nichols.

"The man in the better shape will win the fight and I've never been in better shape in my life," Braddock said. "I would like to say to the boxing fans and to the public at large that I will be in the best shape any athlete can possibly get into for the fight. And it will be some fight. Baer won't be able to take it easy with me. I won't let him. He will have to box fifteen rounds in two, not two in fifteen as he's been doing in his last few bouts. There will be no chance for him to clown, pull up his trunks or wave to the audience. I know what this fight means to me and I will give the public all that is humanly possible to give."

Braddock didn't want to come off as boastful or cocky. In fact, he only said those words after persistent prodding from Nichols, who reported as much in his articles.

If anyone was willing to brag, it was manager Joe Gould.

"Jimmy does not fear Baer," Gould told Nichols. "That's a point in his favour, especially when you consider the last few men to face the champion seemed to have too much respect for him. To Jimmy, it's just another fight. In my experience, I have found that the toughest game is the game of life and when a man can do in that game what Jimmy has done, what does a fight mean? Or a punch to the chin?"

Gould also told Nichols that despite winning or losing, Braddock had received guaranteed appearance offers to fight in England and Ireland. But Gould made one last promise.

"We don't intend on losing," Gould said.

While his fighter was supposedly training to face Braddock, Baer's manager Ancil Hoffman was arranging a post-fight tour across the country, as well as securing Baer bit roles in three motion pictures.

Braddock continued to train rigorously for the fight, working on the strategy he had learned from the Loughran bouts. He never realized that a good, old-fashioned whupping six years earlier would come back to help him.

Gould stressed footwork, speed, quickness. Use the left, over and over. Jab, jab. One writer even whimsically called Braddock by an old nickname, "Jabbin' Jim."

"Don't write that," Gould told the writer. "We don't want Baer to know."

Braddock was asked what it was like to get a chance to fight for the title.

"It's one of those things that happens to you in life," Braddock said. "You're not always in the right spot at the right time. That's the way it is in boxing. You get the breaks and then sometimes, you don't get the breaks. If you get the breaks, then you're in there, getting a shot at the top. If you don't, you're at the bottom. I knew a lot about both places."

At the weigh-in for the fight, Baer tipped the scale at 209 ½ pounds, while Braddock was considerably less, hitting 191 ¾. That was nothing new for Braddock, the size differential. The size, the powerful punch of Baer, the reputation—none of that mattered now. Braddock was ready and he knew it.

The referee for the fight was Johnny McAvoy, a veteran of the boxing game with more than 25 championship fights officiated. The judges were New York boxing experts Charley Lynch and George Kelly.

Jacobs promoted a six-bout card, all heavyweights, that featured boxing fixtures "Two Ton" Tony Galento and Steve Dudas, but the turnout was a disappointing 35,000 at the Madison Square Garden Bowl.

Apparently, there weren't many people who thought Braddock stood a chance, and the doubters stayed away. Because of the disappointing gate, the anticipated windfall that Braddock had hoped to receive, $60,000, was sliced nearly in half, to somewhere around $32,000.

But it wasn't time to worry about gate receipts and financial stability. This was the chance of a lifetime. Braddock was finally fighting for a title again.

Braddock came out and utilized the strategy, leading with the left, from the outset—a move that totally stunned Baer and his corner. In the first round, Braddock hit Baer with a left to the head and followed with a right to the body. Baer missed Braddock with some roundhouse left hooks, but then connected with a left to the body and a combination to Braddock's head. Braddock retaliated with two straight lefts to the head.

In the second round, it was more of the same. Braddock struck Baer with two lefts, then tried one of his patented rights, but he missed the champ, causing the flamboyant Baer to smile widely at his opponent, then flash a grin to the crowd. Braddock then hit Baer with two powerful rights, both to the jaw. Baer came back with a left to the head, then seemed to rush toward Braddock, who was not fazed by the tactic. However, Baer landed a huge left-right combination to Braddock's ribs, obviously hurting him.

"Hitting him with my left hand and moving," Braddock told Heller. "That was on my mind the whole time. I hit him with a few right hands early on, but he landed some on me. He was a dynamite puncher. If he hit you right, you could end up in the third row. He hit me a few times and I yelled at him, 'Is that as hard as you can punch?' I think that took a little out of him."

In the third round, Braddock started off again with two straight left jabs to Baer's face. He then flicked two short left jabs again and tried to follow with a right that Baer defended well. Keeping score on his own, Nichols, at ringside, had Braddock already way ahead on points.

In the fourth round, Braddock and Baer traded left hands, then Braddock hooked a solid left to the head of the champ. Baer was completely surprised that Braddock had such a powerful left hand. Two more jabs to the head caused Baer to clinch with Braddock before McAvoy could step in and break them up, and the crowd issued a chorus of boos. McAvoy warned Baer, who apologized to Braddock, then gestured to the crowd, almost apologetically.

In the fifth round, Baer did something else that infuriated McAvoy: he hit Braddock with the back of his hand. McAvoy issued a warning and the crowd booed again. By this point, the crowd was clearly in Braddock's corner.

Braddock hooked Baer with a hard left that landed right on the champ's jaw. Baer inadvertently backhanded Braddock again, drawing another warning and more ire from the referee. Nichols gave the round to Braddock because of the two warnings.

In the sixth and seventh rounds, Braddock continued to score regularly with the stunning left hand and Baer had no defense or recourse. Braddock then hit Baer with a solid right that caused the champ's knees to buckle. It looked as if Baer might go down. Braddock followed it up with three straight lefts. He was clearly in control—much to the delight of the crowd—but he was also in a state of shock.

In the seventh round, Braddock hit Baer with a tremendous right. In earlier years, that would have been the punch that gave Braddock a victory. But at 29, Braddock didn't have the power in that damaged hand that he'd had when he was 20. Baer took the monstrous right and simply laughed. But it was no joke, because Braddock was winning.

"I said to him, 'Hey, Max, you better get going,' " Braddock said in Heller's book. " 'You're way behind.' I just kept sticking him."

In the ninth round, Baer hit Braddock with an obvious low blow, and a lot of other fighters might have faked an injury to secure the win. But Braddock wasn't going to accept a win that way. He continued on. Baer received yet another infraction warning. Braddock ended the round with two solid left hands.

From the tenth through to the 12th rounds, it was more of a chess match between the two fighters. Gould told Braddock that he was clearly ahead and had to avoid making a fatal mistake that would cost him the fight. The desperate Baer would have to do something radical to steal the fight back from Braddock.

"Right from the eighth or ninth round, I knew it," Braddock told Heller. "Because he wasn't getting any better and I was doing a lot better. I was definitely reaching him with more jabs."

Considering that Braddock had never lost via knockout before—only having endured the technical-knockout loss to Lou Scozza in 1932, when the fight was stopped due to a cut over Braddock's left eye—one would figure that Braddock was not going to get counted out of this fight, especially not with a championship there for the taking.

Baer was frustrated at the end of Round 12 and continued to throw punches after the bell. By now, the crowd was caught up in the fever of rooting for the underdog. Baer hit Braddock with a solid, hard right in Round 13 that shook Braddock a bit, but he didn't waver. Braddock kept the champ at bay in the 14th round with the now-familiar left jab.

Before the 15th round began, the two opponents shook hands. Braddock started with a strong left to the body, then held his ground. The crowd was sensing the upset.

Legendary New York sportswriter Edward J. Neil said that over the last two rounds of the fight, "you could feel the tension increasing, feel breaths shortening, until the hair stood up on the back of your neck."

Braddock had the fight won already, but he didn't stop in the final round, methodically sticking to the same strategy he had from the outset. Braddock withstood one last flurry from Baer, then ended the fight in fitting fashion, with a straight, hard right to Baer's jaw as the bell rang.

In terms of boxing purism, it wasn't one of the greatest fights in boxing history. But in terms of magnitude and importance to sport—and to humanity—there was no bigger moment. Maybe the United States hockey team capturing the gold medal at the 1980 Olympics was as big. Maybe the 1969 New York Mets winning the World Series, or the back-door sweep completed by the 2004 Red Sox against the Yankees on the road to their first title in 86 years.

But this was a man who just nine months before was on welfare, collecting $24 a month. Now, after gaining a unanimous decision over Max Baer, in the greatest upset in the history of boxing, James J. Braddock had attained the unthinkable, the unimaginable. He was the heavyweight champion of the world.

*James Braddock runs along a beach as he trains, Florida, 1936. Braddock became the defending heavyweight champion after winning the title from Max Baer the previous June. (Photo by FPG/Getty Images)*

# 19

Jim Braddock didn't have to wait to hear the judges' decision to know that he had won. Neither did a defeated and demoralized Max Baer, who sat on his stool in total disbelief.

But the decisions were read anyway. Referee Johnny McAvoy scored it nine rounds for Braddock, five for Baer, and one even. Judge Charley Lynch had it 11-4 in favor of Braddock. Judge George Kelly scored it practically even, 7-7-1, but had to give the decision to Braddock because Baer had fouled three times with the low blow and two backhand punches.

It was a unanimous decision. Gould and Braddock hugged for what seemed like an hour. They couldn't believe what had happened, especially after all they had been through.

And both knew that their lives would never be the same.

"I remember it was tougher for me to get back to the dressing room that night than it ever was before," Braddock told Heller. "People were pulling my hair, reaching out for me, grabbing at me. I had bodyguards take me through. They were reaching, just wanting to touch me, to let me know they were there. It was a great night. We got a lot of nice accolades from different people around the country. I'm the happiest guy in the world. Nobody knew what that fight meant to me. Money, security, education for my children, financial aid for my parents. If ever a guy went into the ring with something to fight for, I was the guy."

Edward J. Neil called it "one of the most dramatic moments in the history of the prize ring."

One of the first telegrams Braddock received was from Washington, D.C.

*Mr. Braddock,*

*You represent an entire nation well. In our nation's toughest times, you symbolize what it means to be able to recover from financial disparity and becoming able to rise above and make a name for yourself. We're all proud of your incredible achievement. You will be a role model for so many others who struggled through our Great Depression. Congratulations on your championship and*

*realize that your success is shared by millions of Americans
who look up to you, because you are truly one of them.*
                                    Sincerely, Franklin D. Roosevelt

FDR's wire of well-wishes was far from the last communication that Braddock would receive. In fact, the cards and letters started streaming in from all over the country, from people who didn't know Jim Braddock from a hole in the wall.

A farmer in Kansas wrote to Braddock and told him that he was in financial ruin and had been on the brink of committing suicide, until he tuned in to listen to the Braddock-Baer fight on radio.

"You gave me hope," the letter read. "For that, I thank you. I thought I had no hope."

Some of the letters came from small boys who were beginning to idolize Braddock and were looking for his autograph. But most of the letters were from everyday Americans, who just wanted to relay their own stories to the new king of the boxing world.

John D. McCallum wrote in *The Encyclopedia of World Boxing Champions* that the letters came from "men who had good positions and lost them, whose life savings had been swept away by the Wall Street disaster, whose families were in need; from those who had been alone in the world and who were plodding in a weary way, hopeless until this big guy had come swinging back from obscurity to show them how a losing fight could be won."

It wasn't until Jim Braddock started reading the countless cards and letters that streamed into his family's North Bergen home on a daily basis that he realized the true magnitude of his victory. It wasn't simply about boxing. It was a victory for all of America, for the common man.

After the royalties and radio rights were paid out from the Baer fight, Braddock received a total of $55,000. Considering that this was a man who fought Corn Griffin nine months earlier for a sum of $250, it really was the prototypical "rags to riches" story.

Although Braddock was the champion, everyone in the boxing game knew that the two biggest names and contenders were German Max Schmeling and the "Brown Bomber" from Detroit, the undefeated Joe Louis.

Braddock didn't want to climb back into the ring right away, so he held off any official title defenses. Instead, he was now the one who went on a barnstorming tour to capitalize on his new-found popularity, travelling to box in exhibitions against sparring partner Jack McCarthy, a heavyweight from Boston who had a less-than-distinguished professional career and once lost to old Braddock foe Charley Retzlaff.

Braddock and Gould took McCarthy with them to Columbus, Houston, Seattle, Portland, San Francisco and Oakland, to participate in three-round exhibitions where Braddock received an appearance fee and was able to meet and greet some of his newly avid fans.

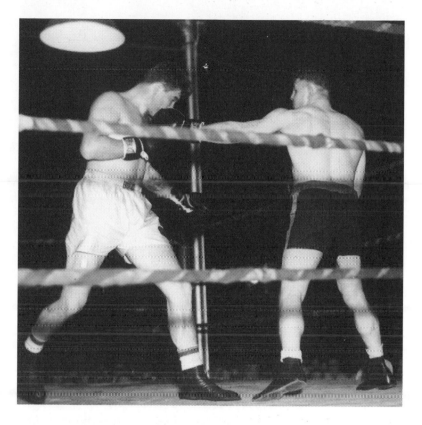

*A month after defeating Max Baer for the heavyweight championship, Braddock (left) fights Tom Patick in a exhibition bout, Jersey City, New Jersey, July 16, 1935. (Photo by FPG/Getty Images)*

Every day, Braddock was gaining more and more popularity as one of the most recognized professional athletes in America, right there with Babe Ruth and Lou Gehrig.

The barnstorming tour took Braddock from July to November of 1935. There were other appearances that came with being the heavyweight champion of the world, like radio spots and photo advertisements.

When Braddock returned home in late November, he simply wanted to spend time with Mae and the kids. After all, the family was no longer in financial distress and Braddock had earned a rest. He would head to the gym to train every so often with Gould, but with no pending bouts on the immediate horizon, Braddock enjoyed some much-deserved time off.

Meanwhile, Louis's star continued to rise. In September, 1935, the Brown Bomber knocked out Max Baer in the fourth round of a fight held before 88,000 spectators at Yankee Stadium in New York. After the fight, it was determined that Baer should have been saved by the bell in the fourth round; that the round actually lasted three minutes and nine seconds, but that didn't stop Louis from going to 25-0 and becoming a very popular figure, despite the colour of his skin.

Schmeling was also making a name for himself overseas, winning impressively over quality boxers like Steve Hamas and Paolino Uzcudun.

In June of 1936, one of the most anticipated bouts in the history of boxing took place—the first meeting between former champ Schmeling and Louis. With a crowd of more than 80,000 in attendance, the unwilling symbol of Nazi supremacy and the African-American squared off at Yankee Stadium. Schmeling came away with a 12th-round knockout, knocking down the previously undefeated Louis in both the 4th and 12th rounds. Louis had been a 4-to-1 favourite.

Because Schmeling had won in convincing fashion, Madison Square Garden promoters worked fast to secure a heavyweight title fight between Schmeling and Braddock, and it was scheduled for September 30, 1936 at Madison Square Garden.

But Braddock pulled out of the fight with three weeks to go due to a hand injury he suffered while training.

At the same time, Gould was working with Louis's manager, Mike Jacobs, on a possible Louis-Braddock fight for the title. Gould, being of Jewish descent, didn't want to see a so-called Nazi get the first crack at Braddock's crown.

"I was going to fight Schmeling, but the Jews in New York, who were great fight fans, were against Schmeling on the account of Hitler," Braddock told Heller. "They weren't going to support the fight and I had a lot of Jewish fans, so that couldn't happen."

After Braddock pulled out of the scheduled fight with Schmeling because of the hand injury, the New York State Athletic Commission held a hearing that said, "The Commission forbids James Braddock from engaging in a bout of any length whatsoever against Joe Louis before he defends his title against Max Schmeling."

But that ruling didn't deter Gould. He was working on one of the most ingenious deals ever struck in boxing, one with Louis's manager Mike Jacobs that would make Braddock financially secure for the rest of his life.

*James Braddock (left), heavyweight champion of the world, and Joe Louis, the challenger, are shown shaking hands after they had signed for their title bout in Chicago. (Photo © Corbis. All rights reserved.)*

# 20

James Lambert Harte wrote a book in 1938 entitled *The Amazing Story of James J. Braddock*. In the book, Harte wrote that "greater fighters than the Jersey Irishman have held the heavyweight championship, but none of them ever made a deeper impression in his time. For Braddock's influence extended far beyond those who never saw a bout, wouldn't go across the street to see one and except for him, had no interest in any prizefighter. The aged and the infirmed and the out of luck, the forgotten victims of the Great Depression that crushed and tormented them."

Braddock had become the archetypal boxing hero in an era when Hollywood was churning out such boxing-based films as *The Champ, Golden Boy, City for Conquest* and *Kid Galahad*.

"In no list that you will ever see will he be listed among the ten greatest, but that is as it should be," legendary boxing writer W.C. Heinz wrote of Braddock. "He may, however, in the sense that others see themselves in him and read their own struggles into his, have belonged to more people than any other champion who ever lived."

In an era when America desperately needed a hero, they found it in Jim Braddock. He was everyman and every man's hero. He was someone the entire country could relate to. Joe Gould wanted to make sure that he was going to be taken care of for the remainder of his life.

So Gould arranged an unprecedented deal with Mike Jacobs, the manager of Joe Louis. If Gould allowed Louis to fight Braddock for the heavyweight title, then Gould wanted 10 percent of all of Louis's heavyweight-championship gate receipts for the next 10 years, if Louis won the fight.

Jacobs didn't think that the deal would ever extend for 10 years, so he agreed to it. He just wanted to get a shot at the title for his fighter.

So Jacobs signed the deal with Braddock and Gould. It was almost like an annuity plan. No matter what happened in the fight, Braddock was going to be financially set. He wouldn't have to fight the German Schmeling, which infuriated some, but pleased many, because there was the fear that with the outbreak of Hitler's Nazi regime,

Schmeling would take the heavyweight title to Germany and never return.

The deal was done. Braddock would defend his title on June 22, 1937 against Louis at Comiskey Park in Chicago. It was almost two years to the day since he defeated Baer to win the title, but Gould and Braddock had to make sure that the timing was right for the proper title defense. Braddock would get 50 percent of the proposed $1 million gate, while Louis got 17 percent.

While there was a heavy anti-Nazi sentiment in the country, there were also still racist feelings against blacks as well. There were some people who were upset that Braddock was going to give a title shot to a black boxer. They believed that the fight game should be ruled by the white man and that the blacks had no place in it.

Braddock was not one to ever see colour, race, creed or religion. After all, he was an Irishman with a Jewish manager. It didn't matter to him that he was going to fight a black man with the title on the line.

There was also one prominent black man who was upset that Louis was getting a chance—namely, the first African-American to win the heavyweight title, Jack Johnson.

Johnson was livid when he found out that Louis was getting a shot at the crown he once held. At every chance he got, Johnson openly criticized Louis and bet heavily on Louis's opponents.

So when the white heavyweight champion Braddock gave Louis a shot at the title, marking the first time a white champion had agreed to fight a black challenger since Tommy Burns fought Johnson and beat him 29 years earlier, Johnson even volunteered to help train Braddock.

Braddock declined Johnson's offer.

There was another obstacle that Braddock had to handle before he entered the ring. Unknown to most in boxing circles, Braddock had been battling arthritis on the left side of his body, his shoulder and ribs, and was on medication for it.

The pain started to develop after the Baer fight, but it wasn't made public. Braddock tried to receive treatment for the pain and also learned to live through it. Hell, this was a man who had broken his right hand five times, broken his nose at least a dozen. He'd had rib problems, more than 50 stitches to his face and an assortment of leg and back woes over the years. A little pain to his side was minuscule.

Braddock was going to enter the ring against Louis at less than 100 per cent.

"I had a doctor taking care of my arm so I could lift it," Braddock said in Heller's book. "The morning of the fight in Chicago, the doctor gave me a shot in the arm so I could lift it. I knew I needed that strong left hand against Louis. Evidently, the stuff he gave me in the shot didn't last long, because I couldn't do much with it against Louis."

For some unknown reason, Braddock didn't fight Louis with the same strategy that he used against Baer. Braddock was told by reporters that Louis looked out of shape and lethargic in his training-camp workouts. Both fighters were

*During an early round of the heavyweight championship bout, Braddock unleashed his famous right hand at Joe Louis' chin. (Photo © Corbis. All rights reserved.)*

photographed and reported on in camp by *Life* magazine. When the writers were around, Louis could barely pick up a medicine ball and seemed to be going through the motions. Those writers then spread that word to Braddock.

However, it was apparently all part of a master ploy by Jacobs, who was getting Louis up at the crack of dawn to run 10 miles a day to get in shape and had his fighter do most of the speed and sparring work in the early morning before the writers arrived. Jacobs was just as shrewd as Gould.

So Braddock came right after Louis from the outset and actually knocked Louis down in the first round.

"He feigned me into him and I didn't go for it," Braddock said in Heller's book. "He bent down low and I had to uppercut Joe and he went down. If he had been standing up and I hit him straight, it might have been a different story. I then missed his chin with a right and hit him in the chest. If I hit him with that right, that might have been it. I figured if I could get a good punch in on the chin, I could take him, because Joe always had a tough time with punches around the face."

However, the aggressive style came back to haunt Braddock.

"For four rounds, I was OK, but then he started to come on and he really went to work on me," Braddock recalled. "From the fourth to the eighth rounds, I got hit with more punches than I got hit with in my prior 87 fights. Because I never got hit much, I never got cut up that bad.

But that night, I got 23 stitches to my face. He hit me in the eighth round and drove one of my teeth through the mouthpiece and right straight through the lip."

Louis systematically destroyed Braddock. It was clearly the worst beating of his career.

"It felt as if someone took a light bulb and jammed it into your face to bust it," Braddock described Louis's punch.

The champ was headed for trouble, and finally in the eighth round, Louis unleashed a barrage that put the soon-to-be former champion to the canvas.

"When he knocked me down, I could have stayed there for three weeks," Braddock told Heller. "You could feel the power the guy had."

Louis knocked Braddock out in the eighth round and captured the heavyweight championship. It was the first and only time ever that Braddock lost by a conventional knockout.

"I'm glad I had the chance to fight the guy, because as it came out, he was one of the greatest fighters in history," Braddock said. "Even though I lost, the fans enjoyed it. It was pure action for eight rounds. Having the championship and then losing it, you always have to figure that you're not the best man in the world, that there's someone out there who's better. That's the way it was. That's the way boxing is. The champion doesn't always stand up at the end. There's always somebody who comes along and is willing to take him. That's a part of life."

*Joe Louis, left, exchanges left jabs with defending heavyweight champion James J. Braddock at Comiskey Park in Chicago, Ill., on June 22, 1937. Louis knocked out Braddock in the eighth round to win the world heavyweight title. (AP Photo)*

Sportswriters praised Braddock's courage against Louis.

"The exhibition of courage the gallant Anglo-Irishman gave before that final bolt of lightning struck him on the side of the jaw awakened admiration and compassion for him in the heart of everyone in that vast crowd," wrote Dan Parker of the *New York Daily Mirror*.

Despite the loss, Braddock's impeccable reputation and legend were helped immensely by the Louis fight.

After the fight, Braddock returned home to North Bergen and pondered his future. He had the $500,000 he received from the Louis fight, and he was slated to receive as much as $150,000 from Louis over the next 10 years, courtesy of Gould's unique arrangement.

Braddock still had his fame and popularity. He tried to open a sports bar and grill in midtown Manhattan, just like his friend Jack Dempsey had. The place, located on West 49th Street, was called "Inn Braddock's Corner," which was a great idea, except for one thing. Braddock was such a nice man that he constantly gave away drinks. The business failed after a few years. Gould was the vice president of the restaurant.

Braddock also tried his hand at radio broadcasting, having read the script of *The Case of the Jersey Butcher Bandits* on the popular radio show *Gangbusters*, on New Year's Day, 1938.

After losing to Louis, Braddock stayed in the fight game for one more fight, taking on Tommy Farr of Wales, the

British boxing champion who had won 18 straight fights before losing to Louis in August of 1937.

Again, Braddock was in the familiar role of heavy underdog when he took on Farr at Madison Square Garden on January 21, 1938 in a six-bout card that also featured Braddock's sparring partner from the barnstorming tour, Jack McCarthy. In typical fashion, the underdog won, gaining a close split decision. One judge had it 6-4 Braddock, the other had it 6-4 Farr. Referee Johnny McAvoy, the same ref who did the Braddock-Baer fight, had it 4-4-2, with Braddock ahead on points. It was that close, but a win all the same. And the perfect way to bid farewell—with one final comeback.

"Farr had given Joe Louis a good, tough fight," Braddock said. "I held my own, but I found out in the last three rounds that I couldn't back up anymore. I could go forward all right, but I couldn't back up. I was really worried that I could have gotten hurt. I got back to the dressing room after the fight and Gould knew already what I was thinking. I said, 'That's it.' I could have been out there a little while longer, making a good payday, but I could have also been hurt and come out a cripple. I figured I had to get out while the going was good."

Two days after the fight with Farr, Braddock officially announced his retirement from boxing. He was 32 years old.

"Although I won my last fight and I think I could still beat most of the outstanding contenders out there, I've fought my last fight," Braddock told reporters on January

30, 1938. "I've spent fifteen years in this game and in fairness to everyone, especially my wife and children, I believe it's time for me to withdraw."

Braddock walked away from the game, even though Mike Jacobs had arranged a $100,000 guarantee for a rematch with Max Baer and a $50,000 for a rematch with Tommy Farr. Braddock didn't need more money. He had enough.

"You have to like it to be in there," Braddock told Heller. "That's definitely one business you have to like if you're going to be in it."

Braddock retired with a less-than-stellar professional record of 51 victories and 26 losses, with seven draws and two no-contests. It is by far the highest loss total of any heavyweight champion in boxing history.

Braddock did manage to go back into the ring one more time on March 26, 1941, in an exhibition bout against Clarence "Red" Burman in Charlotte, North Carolina, in a fundraiser to help those who were still trying to recover from losses suffered in the Great Depression.

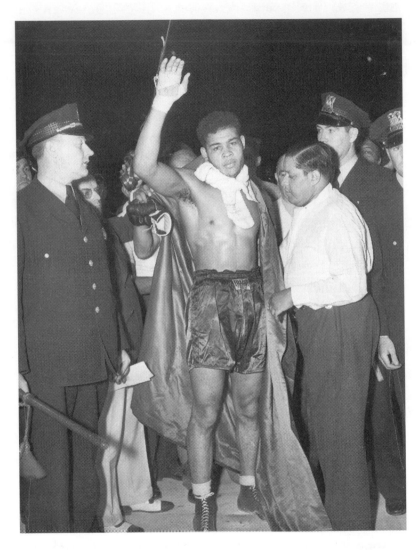

*Joe Louis, with hand upraised, is pronounced the new heavyweight champion of the world, after his eighth round knockout of Jimmy Braddock in Chicago. June 22, 1937. (Photo © Corbis. All rights reserved.)*

# 21

After Jim Braddock officially announced his retirement from boxing in January of 1938, he quickly began to map out what he planned to do for the rest of his life. He had already ventured into the restaurant world, although that investment didn't turn out as well as Jack Dempsey's restaurant, which remained a social staple of the New York theatre district for four decades.

He also owned a taxicab service that failed as well, but then he got involved in the airline business, eventually becoming a marine equipment surplus supplier, concentrating on generators and welding equipment. That business was highly successful, and Braddock focused on becoming a good businessman.

Even in retirement, Braddock maintained a positive relationship with Gould. He hired Gould to help run his restaurant and the two worked together in the marine equipment business, right up until World War II, when the two enlisted together in the United States Army.

Although Braddock and Gould never saw action in the army, Braddock was very influential in the sale of war bonds to help the cause of the military. In fact, Braddock and Joe Louis, who also enlisted, served together on a war-bond selling tour.

The friendship of Braddock and Louis remained strong over the years. James Braddock III, the champ's grandson, said that he remembered his father telling stories of walking into the family living room in North Bergen and seeing people like Jack Dempsey and Joe Louis sitting and talking with Braddock.

In fact, Braddock became a great ambassador for the sport. He would constantly make appearances at heavyweight-championship fights, including doing some impromptu television broadcasting at the Muhammad Ali-Sonny Liston fight in Lewiston, Maine in 1965, sharing the microphone with Howard Cosell.

Braddock was also seen regularly at the boxing cards near his home in North Bergen. There was a traditional Friday Night Fights Card at a boxing facility called Embassy Hall in North Bergen, and Braddock was often the master of ceremonies for those weekly affairs.

The relationship between Braddock and Gould soured

somewhat in 1944, when, as a captain in the Army and director of athletic facilities at Camp Shanks in New York, Gould was convicted by general court martial of conspiracy to defraud the federal government in the awarding of contracts for army equipment. The original sentence of three years in prison and $12,000 in fines was reduced to a year in prison and a $1,000 fine. However, Gould was dismissed from the military for his actions.

Gould died in 1952 of undisclosed causes in New York. He was 53 years old.

Braddock never wanted to leave his home of North Bergen. He was comfortable in the home that he bought with the earnings he received from the Max Baer fight, and he raised his three children there with his loving wife, Mae.

The home on 79th Street in North Bergen was located directly across the street from a park where Braddock spent many of his elder days watching children play. In fact, neighbors said that they used to watch Braddock go into the park on a daily basis and play with the children. He always loved to be close to home, and he always loved children.

While boxers like Max Baer and Maxie Rosenbloom sought fame in the entertainment world of Hollywood, Braddock was content to remain at home with Mae and the children.

As he grew older, the accolades began to come in for Braddock. He was named to *The Ring* magazine's Boxing Hall of Fame in 1964, an honour he relished.

"When I was being considered a bum, no one would

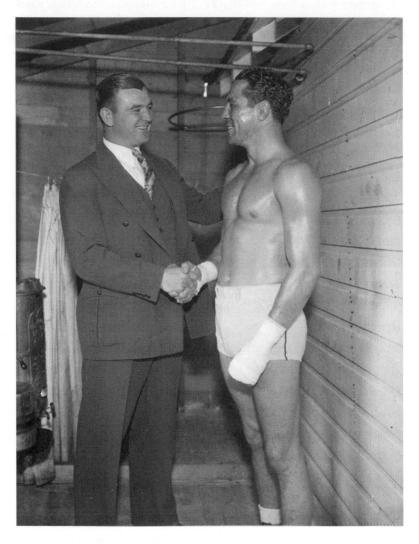

*Braddock (left) shakes hands with Max Baer, the former champion, to wish him luck for his bout with Joe Louis at Yankee Stadium. (Photo © Corbis. All rights reserved.)*

have ever picked me to be a Hall of Famer," Braddock said on the night of his induction. "This is one of the greatest moments of my life."

On November 29, 1974, at the age of 68, James Walter Braddock, also known as James J. Braddock, Gentle Jim, Jersey James, Jabbin' Jim, and last but not least, The Cinderella Man, died in his sleep in his North Bergen home. He left his wife, three children, four brothers, two sisters, and six grandchildren.

A few years after his passing, the park across the street from his home, where he watched the children of the neighbourhood play and where he joined in, was renamed from North Hudson Park to North Hudson Braddock Park in his honour.

In 1991, Braddock was inducted posthumously into the first class ever of the Hudson County Sports Hall of Fame. Ten years later, he received the ultimate honour, when he was inducted into the International Boxing Hall of Fame.

Now, some 30 years after his death, the Cinderella Man is about to become part of America's lexicon once again, thanks to the movie by Universal Pictures.

It's safe to say that no one will ever forget the Cinderella Man.

# JAMES J. BRADDOCK'S
# FIGHT RECORD

| DATE | OPPONENT | RESULT |
|---|---|---|
| 1926 | | |
| Apr 14 | Al Settle | ND 4 |
| Apr 22 | George Deschner | KO 2 |
| May | Phil Weisberger | KO 1 |
| May | Jack O'Day | KO 1 |
| May | Willie Daily | KO 1 |
| Jun 18 | Leo Dobson | KO 1 |
| Jul 9 | Walter Westman | TK 3 |
| Aug | Jim Pearson | KO 2 |
| Aug | Gene Travers | KO 1 |
| Sep 13 | Mike Rock | KO 1 |
| Sep 16 | Ray Kennedy | KO 1 |
| Sep 30 | Carmine Caggiano | KO 1 |
| Nov 12 | Lou Barba | W 6 |
| Dec 4 | Al Settle | W 6 |
| Dec 8 | Joe Hudson | W 6 |
| Dec 20 | Doc Conrad | ND 4 |
| 1927 | | |
| Jan 28 | George LaRocco | KO 1 |
| Feb 1 | Johnny Alberts | KO 4 |
| Feb 15 | Jack Nelson | W 6 |
| Mar 3 | Lou Barba | W 4 |
| Mar 8 | Nick Fadil | W 6 |
| Mar | Tom McKiernan | KO 2 |
| Apr 19 | Frankie Lennon | KO 3 |
| May 2 | Stanley Simmons — Weight Class: 170 - 180 | TK 1 |
| May 11 | Jack Stone | ND 10 |

163

# Jim Hague

| DATE | OPPONENT | RESULT |
|------|----------|--------|
| May 20 | George LaRocco | D 6 |
| May 27 | Paul Cavalier | ND 10 |
| Jun 8 | Jimmy Francis—Weight Class: 168 - 169 | ND 10 |
| Jul 13 | Jimmy Francis | ND 10 |
| Jul 21 | George LaRocco—Weight Class: 165 1/2 - 179 | W 6 |
| Aug 10 | Vic McLaughlin | ND 10 |
| Sep 21 | Herman Heller | ND 10 |
| Oct 5 | Joe Monte | D 10 |
| **1928** | | |
| Jan 6 | Paul Swiderski | W 8 |
| May 7 | Jack Darnell | KO 4 |
| May 16 | Jimmy Francis | ND 10 |
| Jun 7 | Joe Monte | L 10 |
| Jun 27 | Billy Vidabeck | ND 10 |
| Jul 25 | Nando Tassi | D 10 |
| Aug 8 | Joe Sekyra | L 10 |
| Oct 17 | Pete Latzo | W 10 |
| Nov 30 | Gerald "Tuffy" Griffith | KO 2 |
| **1929** | | |
| Jan 18 | Leo Lomski | L 10 |
| Feb 4 | George Gemas | KO 1 |
| Mar 11 | Jimmy Slattery | TK 9 |
| Apr 22 | Eddie Benson | KO 1 |
| Jul 18 | Tommy Loughran—Light Heavyweight Championship of the World | L 15 |
| Aug 27 | Yale Okun | L 10 |
| Nov 15 | Max Rosenbloom | L 10 |
| Dec 7 | Jack "Jake" Warren | KO 2 |
| **1930** | | |
| Jan 17 | Leo Lomski | L 10 |
| Apr 7 | Billy Jones | L 10 |
| Jun 5 | Harold Mays | ND 10 |
| Jul 2 | Joe Monte | W 10 |
| Aug 12 | Alvin "Babe" Hunt | L 10 |
| Sep 19 | Phil Mercurio | KO 2 |

| DATE | OPPONENT | RESULT |
|------|----------|--------|
| **1931** | | |
| Jan 23 | Ernie Schaaf | L 10 |
| Mar 5 | Jack Roper | KO 1 |
| Mar 30 | Jack Kelly | W 10 |
| Sep 3 | Andy Mitchell | D 10 |
| Oct 9 | Joe Sekyra | L 10 |
| Nov 10 | Max Rosenbloom | NC 2 |
| Dec 4 | Al Gainer | L 10 |
| **1932** | | |
| Mar 18 | Baxter Calmes | L 10 |
| May 13 | Charley Retzlaff | L 10 |
| Jun 21 | Vincent Parille | W 5 |
| Jul 25 | Tony Shucco | L 8 |
| Sep 21 | John Henry Lewis | L 10 |
| Sep 30 | Dynamite Jackson | W 10 |
| Oct 21 | Tom Patrick | L 10 |
| Nov 9 | Lou Scozza | LT 6 |
| **1933** | | |
| Jan 13 | Martin Levandowski | W 10 |
| Jan 20 | Hans Birkie | L 10 |
| Mar 1 | Al Ettore | LF 4 |
| Mar 21 | Al Stillman | TK 10 |
| Apr 5 | Martin Levandowski | L 10 |
| May 19 | Al Stillman | L 10 |
| Jun 21 | Les Kennedy | W 10 |
| Jul 21 | Chester Matan | W 10 |
| Sep 25 | Abe Feldman | NC 8 |
| **1934** | | |
| Jun 14 | John "Corn" Griffin | TK 3 |
| Nov 16 | John Henry Lewis | W 10 |
| **1935** | | |
| Mar 22 | Art Lasky | W 15 |
| Jun 13 | Max Baer—Heavyweight Championship of the World | W 15 |
| Jul 18 | Jack McCarthy | EX 3 |
| Aug 27 | Jack McCarthy | EX 3 |

**165**

*Jim Hague*

| DATE | OPPONENT | RESULT |
|------|----------|--------|
| Nov 5 | Jack McCarthy | EX 3 |
| Nov 12 | Jack McCarthy | EX 2 |
| Nov 15 | Jack McCarthy | EX 3 |
| Nov 20 | Jack McCarthy | EX 3 |
| 1937 | | |
| Jun 22 | Joe Louis-Heavyweight Championship of the World | LK 8 |
| 1938 | | |
| Jan 21 | Tommy Farr | W 10 |
| 1941 | | |
| Mar 26 | Clarence "Red" Burman | EX 5 |

# Sources

*The following sources were used as references for this book:*

**Books**
*James J. Braddock, the Cinderella Man*, by B. R. Bearden
*The Cinderella Man—James J. Braddock*, by Dr. Joe de Beauchamp
*In This Corner*, by Peter Heller, published by Robson Books

**Newspapers and Magazines**
"Jersey James," by John Kieran, published in *The New York Times*, 1935
"Sports of the Times," by John Kieran, published in *The*

*New York Times*, 1935

"Lucky Jim," by John Kieran, published in *The New York Times*, 1935

"King of the Ring," by Ed Dunn, published in *The Buffalonian*, 1945

"Tommy Loughran, Boxing Master of Yore," by Ted Carroll, published in *The Ring Magazine*, 1958

**Web Sites**

The Cyber Boxing Zone—www.cyberboxingzone.com

Boxrec—www.boxrec.com

Hickok Sports.com—www.hickoksports.com

# About the Author

**J**IM HAGUE has been a professional sportswriter for 22 years, writing for the *Newark Star-Ledger* for the last nine. Hague has written on a wide variety of sports and has covered the New Jersey Nets and the New York Knicks as a regular beat writer, in addition to following both high school and college sports. A winner of several New Jersey Press Association and North Jersey Press Club awards for sportswriting, Hague has also had stints with the *Morristown Daily Record*, the *Woodbridge News Tribune*, the *Hudson Dispatch* and the *North Jersey Herald & News*.

Hague is a lifelong resident of Hudson County, New Jersey. Currently residing in Kearny with his wife, Mary Costello, Hague, who attended Marquette University and majored in journalism, is an avid fan of both the New York Mets and the St. Louis Rams.